THE TIMES

C000163684

QUEEN ELIZABETH II

IN CELEBRATION OF HER NINETIETH BIRTHDAY

6 OUR QUEEN
AN INTIMATE PORTRAIT

As our longest-serving monarch reaches her ninetieth birthday, Sally Bedell Smith admires the Queen's unique combination of duty, humility, courage and humour

10 BORN TO SERVE
THE YOUNG PRINCESS

A royal childhood; Princess Elizabeth's war effort; an enduring love; the death of King George VI; the Coronation; her guiding faith; Prince Philip, her strength and stay

38 QUEEN AND COUNTRY
THE HEAD OF STATE

Her Majesty's government; the hats, the gowns, the bright colours; a world-class diplomat; the head of the Commonwealth; a visit to The Times

70 FAMILY AFFAIR
MOTHER, SISTER, GRANDMOTHER

A monarch and a mummy; the Queen, her sister and their mother; the annus horribilis; Diana, the daughter-in-law; one great granny; George and Charlotte — the future

92 ROYAL LIFE
THE EVERYDAY MONARCH

The Queen at home; the royal residences; hounds of love; the working Queen; the racing demon; a day at the garden party

110 THE LEGACY
A NEW ELIZABETHAN AGE

Reinventing the monarchy; an ear for music; captured on canvas; why Britain's most successful monarch will be such a hard act to follow

ABOUT THE CONTRIBUTORS

SALLY BEDELL SMITH is a bestselling biographer whose subjects include the Queen and Diana, Princess of Wales

THE VERY REV DR IAN BRADLEY is principal of St Mary's College, University of St Andrews, and author of *God Save the Queen: The Spiritual Dimension of Monarchy*

RACHEL CAMPBELL-JOHNSTON has been chief art critic of *The Times* since 2002

DANIEL FINKELSTEIN was made a life peer in 2013, and writes a weekly political column for *The Times*

VALENTINE LOW is royal correspondent of *The Times*

BEN MACINTYRE is a historian and *Times* columnist and a bestselling author of books on espionage

RICHARD MORRISON is chief music critic and culture writer of *The Times*

ANNA MURPHY is fashion director of *The Times*

JULIAN MUSCAT wrote on racing for *The Times* for 17 years and is the author of *Her Majesty's Pleasure: How Horseracing Enthrals the Queen*

SIR PETER STOTHARD was editor of *The Times*, 1992-2002, and of the *TLS*, 2002-2016

HUGO VICKERS is a writer and broadcaster whose books include biographies of the Queen Mother, the Duchess of Windsor and Princess Andrew of Greece

GILES WHITTELL is a former Washington bureau chief for *The Times*, and now the paper's chief leader writer

DAMIAN WHITWORTH is a *Times* feature writer and interviewer

KATE WILLIAMS is a royal historian and broadcaster and the author of *Young Elizabeth: The Making of Our Queen*

Editor
Bridget Harrison
Design
Peter Robertson, Matt Brown, Emma Woodroofe, Isabelle Emmerich
Picture research
Margaret Clark, Kerry Grainger, Lucy Daley, Matthew Brown
With thanks to
Jeremy Farr, Vicki Reeve, Odile Thomas, Helen Lawson, Isabella Bengoechea, Thomas Calvocoressi, Diana Hargreaves, Tim Arbabzadah, Molly Flemming, Elizabeth Perlman, Luke Sale

Cover
The Queen visits a new maternity ward at the Lister Hospital in Stevenage, 2012

◀ **Glorious reign**
On a tour of Cheshire in 1968

Back cover
The Queen and Prince Philip at Windsor Castle in 1959

THE QUEEN AT NINETY

Our Queen
An intimate portrait

She is renowned for her unwavering sense of duty and humility, but the longest-serving British monarch also has a down-to-earth attitude — and a wicked sense of humour, writes Sally Bedell Smith

She may project an image of sombre propriety, but the Queen finds joy in the smallest things. During the 2014 Commonwealth Games in Glasgow she approached two girls in the South Africa swimming team. "Have you been swimming?" she asked. "Oh yes, Ma'am," they replied. "We just won the 100m relay! It was amazing." "I love that word," the Queen told her aides afterwards. "Amazing," she said. "Amazing," she repeated, this time with a slight South African accent.

As the longest-serving monarch in British history, the Queen has reached another impressive milestone, with her 90th birthday on April 21. She is remarkably fit, physically and mentally, and even hacks out on her fell ponies at Windsor Castle when time permits. Last year she undertook 306 engagements at home and 35 abroad. She continues to attend to her daily boxes of government documents and meetings with officials. "She is very much in control," said a senior adviser. "She has her hand on the tiller very firmly and she knows the details of things, yet she is not controlling. She is flexible and very good at delegating."

Elizabeth is imbued with an unwavering sense of duty — Winston Churchill, her first prime minister, told his daughter Mary Soames he was impressed that "she always paid attention to whatever she was doing" — and her thorough training gave her an understanding of the world and the role she would play. Yet the private Queen — Lilibet to her family — is more notable for her spontaneity. She has a great sense of humour, a well-reported gift for mimicry, sharp opinions, physical courage and a kind and generous spirit.

In most official engagements the Queen's traditionally dour demeanour masks the mischievous side of her personality in an effort to preserve the dignity of her role. It was an instinct honed in childhood by her formidable paternal grandmother, Queen Mary, who felt it was inappropriate for a monarch to smile in public.

If the monarch is required to be serious, Elizabeth also insists on being prepared. On the eve of her 40th year on the throne in 1992, she said: "I have a feeling that in the end, probably, training is the answer to a great many things. You can do a lot if you are properly trained, and I hope I have been." Her 12 British prime ministers, even if sceptical at first, have recognised how conscientious she is. Luminaries who meet her in confidential audiences learn that, keeping herself above politics, she can absorb information without a filter of ideology.

The Queen will long be celebrated for her incredible decades of service, meeting thousands of people a year yet not once seeming impatient or bored. How she achieves this will always remain part of her great mystique.

"One gets crafty after a while and learns how to save oneself," she told Jacqueline Kennedy during the First Lady's visit to Buckingham Palace in 1965. Years later, one of the Queen's relatives asked her what she meant. "I have a knack," she said. "As soon as I stop working, I get into the car and I just switch off." That ability to compartmentalise developed at an early age when she would imagine herself as a pony or a horse. "When someone called her and she didn't answer right away," recalled her cousin Lady Mary Clayton, "she would then say, 'I couldn't answer you as a pony.'"

During a state visit to Washington in 1991, Benedicte Valentiner, who oversaw the president's guest quarters, watched the Queen standing alone as she prepared for the day's engagements. "It was as if she were looking inward, getting set," Valentiner said. "This was how she wound up her batteries. There was no chitchat, but standing absolutely still and waiting, resting in herself."

Her training owes much to the influence of key figures in her formative years. Her mother, Queen Elizabeth, promoted discipline by encouraging her to write a diary each night. It became a lifelong habit, "like scrubbing your teeth", the Queen once said. "It's not really a diary like Queen Victoria's, you know ... or as detailed as that. It's quite small." Her mother also impressed on her daughter the maxim that "if you find something or somebody a bore, the fault lies in you". She demonstrated how to walk at a measured pace as well as how to sit at a slight distance from the chair back for hours.

The Queen has perfected a sturdy stance too, which she described to Susan Crosland, the wife of the foreign secretary Anthony Crosland, by hitching her evening gown above her ankles and saying: "Always keep them parallel. Make sure your weight is evenly distributed. That's all there is to it."

She found an early appetite for current events by reading *The Children's Newspaper* as a child. During long walks at Balmoral, Sandringham and Windsor, her father gave her advice and shared his views on government and politics. She watched him reading his daily dispatch boxes of government papers, a habit she has followed throughout her reign every day except Christmas and Easter. She even reads them when she stays with friends for the weekend. Once, when she had been desk-bound for an entire Saturday morning, a friend asked: "Must you, Ma'am?" To which the Queen replied: "I'm afraid if I missed once I would never catch up again."

And yet, behind that doggedness lies her light-hearted spirit. As she was chatting to the soprano Laura Wright at a Buckingham Palace reception two years ago, the Queen unexpectedly performed a snippet of *Sing*, which had been composed by Gary Barlow for her Diamond Jubilee. Guests were taken aback, and the news spread across Twitter. However, those who knew her best would have recalled that the Queen often entertained them with medleys of show tunes, accompanied by her sister, Princess Margaret, at the piano, or belted out songs while perched atop a wooden box during a picnic in the Outer Hebrides.

On her desk in Windsor Castle, Elizabeth keeps one of the "Solar Queen" statuettes popularised by her Diamond Jubilee. "It drives me mad," she told her cousin Lady Elizabeth Anson with a laugh. "The sun comes out and it goes 'click, click, click' and I see myself waving to me!"

Disconcertingly irreverent, her deadpan humour sometimes takes a moment to register its impact. In 2003 her lady-in-waiting Virginia Airlie celebrated her 70th birthday at Annabel's, where the Queen was seated next to Robert Gascoyne-Cecil, the 7th Marquess of Salisbury. The next day the Queen had an engagement at St Albans Cathedral. As she was being introduced to dignitaries by the dean of St Albans, he spotted Lord Salisbury and

◀ **Royal watchers**
Previous page, left:
the royal couple at
Badminton, 1968

◀ **Jewel in the crown**
Previous page, right:
Princess Elizabeth, 1951

▶ **We are amused**
The Queen watches
her horse Balmoral
Fashion compete
at the Royal Windsor
Horse Show in
the Home Park in
May 2015

▶ **Riding with Ronnie**
On horseback in the
Home Park, Windsor,
with President Reagan,
June 1982

◀ **Meet and greet**
Accepting flowers from
well-wishers during
a walkabout to mark
her Silver Jubilee
in June 1977

asked whether she knew him. "Oh yes! Robert and I were in a nightclub last night till half past one."

Guests instantly relax in her presence. President Reagan and his wife, Nancy, arrived for breakfast on a small terrace outside the Queen's bedroom at Windsor Castle in 1982 and encountered unexpected informality. "Lined up on a table were boxes of cereal," recalled Nancy Reagan. "I said to Prince Charles, 'What do I do?' He said, 'Just help yourself.'" Afterwards, the Queen and the president took their famous horse ride together through the Home Park. At one point Reagan was waving so much to onlookers that the Queen worried he might ride straight into a canal next to the Thames. Reagan described her as "in charge of that animal".

For a royal, she can be engagingly down to earth. While at a shoot on a friend's estate in 2001, a wounded cock-pheasant flew out of a hedge straight at her, flapping and clawing, and knocked her down. There was blood on her clothing from the bird's scratches and a detective standing near by feared

she had been shot. He threw himself on top of her and began giving her mouth-to-mouth resuscitation. "I consider we got to know each other rather well," she said and hired the man for her protection force.

On one occasion, in 1995, she invited the artist Frolic Weymouth to lunch in her private dining room at Windsor Castle. To Weymouth's amazement, not only did the Queen insist on serving him from a sideboard, she cleared the table as well. "She stacked the plates," he recalled. She is similarly attentive to her overnight guests. At Balmoral, she shows them to their rooms, where she selects books to their liking.

The Queen's physical courage is an equally unappreciated trait. On June 13, 1981, dressed in the scarlet tunic of the Welsh Guards and her navy-blue riding skirt, she was leading her annual birthday parade up The Mall, riding side-saddle on Burmese, her 19-year-old mare. As she turned towards Horse Guards Parade for the start of Trooping the Colour, six shots rang out from the crowd. Her startled

horse cantered forward. There was pandemonium around her, but she focused entirely on calming Burmese, leaning down to pat the horse's neck and proceeding serenely at a walk. The shots were only blanks, but the Queen later revealed that in a split-second she had seen the man in the crowd pointing the gun and couldn't believe her eyes.

Perhaps her most unlikely quality is her humility. At a party at St James's Palace given by one of her cousins shortly before Prince William's wedding, the Queen made her way there on her own, without any attendants clearing the way for her or making introductions. "She can uphold the identity of herself as Queen and still be humble," said Rhodes. "Her inner modesty stops her getting spoilt."

There remains plenty of pomp and protocol for formal occasions, but in private — when she will "sidle into a room", as one of her private secretaries put it, or slip into the background when someone else is being celebrated — her unaffected humility is what gives Queen Elizabeth II a special grandeur.

BORN TO SERVE
THE YOUNG PRINCESS

Princess Elizabeth, centre left, waves to the crowd from the balcony at Buckingham Palace after the Coronation of her father, George VI, on May 12, 1937. Her mother, Queen Elizabeth, stands on her right, and her sister, Princess Margaret, on her left, with the new King

A ROYAL CHILDHOOD

Princess Elizabeth enjoyed an idyllic, outdoorsy existence with loving parents and her dear sister until the Abdication thrust her into preparation for life on the throne, says Kate Williams

▲ Close-knit
Princess Elizabeth
with her mother,
Queen Elizabeth,
and her sister,
Princess Margaret,
in 1940

▶ Hobby horse
Princess Elizabeth
and Princess
Margaret in 1932.
The future Queen
had about thirty
toy horses

On December 10, 1936, the ten-year-old Princess Elizabeth of York was at home at No 145 Piccadilly with her sister, Margaret. Preparing to write up her notes from her swimming lesson, she heard shouts of "God save the King" from outside. She realised that people were calling for her father. She asked a footman for the reason for the noise. He told her — and she dashed straight up the stairs to Margaret. "Uncle David is going away and isn't coming back, and Papa is going to be King."

"Does that mean you will have to be the next Queen?" demanded Margaret, only six.

"Yes, some day," said her sister.

"Poor you," replied Margaret.

Elizabeth was unruffled. As she would do throughout her life at moments of crisis, she maintained her routine. According to the diary of her governess Marion Crawford, she sat down and began to write up her notes

from the swimming lesson. She wrote at the top of the paper: Abdication Day.

Elizabeth Alexandra Mary was born in the early hours of April 21, 1926, at 17 Bruton Street in Mayfair, the home of her mother's family. She was immediately everybody's favourite. "We have long wanted a child to make our happiness complete," wrote her father, Albert, or "Bertie", Duke of York. The King and Queen, stiff and even unforgiving with their own children, were delighted by their "little darling", who was third in line to the throne at birth. She was named after her mother, great-grandmother and grandmother — consorts rather than queens regnant. "He says nothing about Victoria," George V reported of his son. "I hardly think it necessary." In other words, she didn't need the name of the great female monarch because she would never be Queen.

Although never intended to reign, little

"Lilibet" was catapulted into the full glare of media attention. One newspaper dubbed her "the world's best-known baby". "It almost frightens me that the people love her so much," said her mother, the Duchess of York. "I hope she will be worthy of it." However, the princess was most cherished by the King. She called him Grandpa England.

When Margaret was born, in Scotland in August 1930, Elizabeth was thrilled. "I have got a new baby sister," she told an estate tenant. "She is so very lovely." The Yorks were now "we four" or "us four", surprisingly close for the standards of the time, giggling together at bedtime in their new Piccadilly home. The property was huge by modern standards — with a lift and a ballroom — but it was a house, rather than a palace. Elizabeth and Margaret played in the gardens with the daughters of the neighbours — businessmen and doctors, rather than royals. The two

▲ **A future queen**
Newspapers dubbed
Princess Elizabeth
"the world's
best-known baby"

◀ **The little princess**
Elizabeth, shown
here in 1932, took
ballet lessons after
her studies

▼ **Horse mad**
The Queen's love of
horses has endured
throughout her life

◀ We four
King George
VI and Queen
Elizabeth with
Princess Elizabeth
and Princess
Margaret in the
grounds of Windsor
Castle in 1936

sisters were cared for by the nannies Clara Knight and Margaret (or "Bobo") Macdonald, who kept them to a strict routine of meals, naps and airings.

The sisters played very different roles in the family. Elizabeth was conscientious, striving, dutiful — and so orderly that she couldn't sleep if her shoes were not parallel under her bed. Margaret was spirited and naughty — as she grew older, she blamed every fault on her invented "Cousin Halifax". The duke remarked on Elizabeth's perfectionism and indulged Margaret's silly games.

The duchess wanted her daughters to have "a really happy childhood ... and later, happy marriages". She was not a believer in too much education. The duke had been bullied at school and agreed to a light timetable. All King George wished for was that they develop a "decent hand" — because, he said, "none of my children could write properly".

Crawford came from Edinburgh to be the princesses' governess in 1933. She arrived to find the seven-year-old Elizabeth in bed, pretending to drive her horses, tying her dressing gown cords to the bedsteads. "I mostly go once or twice round the park before I sleep,

you know," she said. Horse mad, the little girl had thirty or so toy horses. Every night they were fed and watered and lined up neatly outside the nursery. The girls began their day bouncing on their parents' bed. Elizabeth had lessons from 9.30am until 11am with Crawford. The rest of the day was passed in exercise, dancing, singing, a short rest and an hour in which "Crawfie" read to her. The princesses played with their mother before supper and enjoyed card games before bed. Queen Mary thought Elizabeth needed more history, but the Yorks preferred their daughters to be running about outside.

In 1936 everything changed. "It was plain to everyone that there was a sudden shadow over the house," Crawford wrote. Elizabeth's grandfather died within a year of his Silver Jubilee. At the end of the year Edward, Prince of Wales, abdicated to marry Wallis Simpson and Elizabeth's father, poor, unprepossessing Bertie, had to become George VI.

"I was overwhelmed," the new King said. Unlike his brother, however, he had a trump card in a perfect little family.

Elizabeth was destined now for quite a different future. She was heir to the throne. Elizabeth attended her father's Coronation in

1937. She sat with Queen Mary and Margaret and took a keen interest in proceedings. "I thought it all very, very wonderful," she wrote in a little book she made for her parents.

The family had to leave their Piccadilly home for the cavernous and rather gloomy Buckingham Palace. Crawfie compared it to "camping in a museum" and Lilibet thought it so big that "people need bicycles". There were dozens of staff and police detectives on guard. The new King and Queen no longer had the time to play every day with their children, but the Queen tried to give her daughters a "normal" childhood, arranging the 1st Buckingham Palace Girl Guides pack, with an attached set of Brownies for the girls. Elizabeth and Margaret practised semaphore in the palace corridors and cooked sausages over fires in the gardens.

Queen Mary's enthusiasm for history finally won the day. In 1938 Elizabeth was sent to Eton twice a week to learn constitutional history from the provost of the school, Henry Marten. As they ploughed through the constitutional scholarship of Sir William Anson, Marten told her that the British monarchy's strength was its adaptability — and he talked of the importance of broadcasting. As he saw it, speaking directly to the subjects via the radio encouraged their loyalty. It was a useful lesson for Elizabeth, who would go on to become an accomplished broadcaster.

The war changed everything for "us four". The girls moved to Windsor, Elizabeth begging her father for a greater role. Her work with the Auxiliary Territorial Service was vital to war propaganda — and throughout her life she has felt a special bond with war veterans. After the war the 19-year-old princess was flung once more into the public eye. Her days were taken up with correspondence and public engagements — opening factories, presenting prizes, addressing delegations and Girl Guides — as well as being colonel of the Grenadier Guards.

The palace did, however, turn down the offer of an honorary degree from Cambridge University. It wouldn't do for the princess to seem too intellectual.

For her 21st birthday Elizabeth received a car from her parents with the numberplate HRH1. On the day itself she was in South Africa on tour. She gave a speech on the radio to the Empire and Commonwealth. As she said: "I can make my solemn act of dedication with a whole Empire listening." Her dedication was one of self-sacrifice and duty. People all over the world listened as she said: "I declare before you all that my whole life, whether it be long or short, shall be devoted to your service."

She was ready to be Queen.

▶ **Taking flight**
Elizabeth and her younger sister, Margaret, joined the 1st Buckingham Palace pack of Girl Guides; here, they release a pigeon

▶ **At your service**
The teenage princess, pictured here in 1943, studied constitutional history to prepare for her new destiny

THE ARMY DRIVER

Elizabeth was desperate to help the war effort, and she proved a propaganda hit, says Valentine Low

On the evening of September 3, 1939, King George VI broadcast to the nation: "For the second time in the lives of most of us, we are at war." Princess Elizabeth and Princess Margaret sat close to the wireless in Scotland, listening. Elizabeth was 13.

The princesses remained in Scotland until after Christmas, when they moved to Royal Lodge then Windsor Castle. The King and Queen lived at Buckingham Palace and refused to listen to government pleas that they should escape to Canada or the United States. As the Queen said: "The children will not leave unless I do. I shall not leave until their father does, and the King will not leave the country under any circumstances whatsoever."

In Windsor the children continued lessons, ate their rations in darkness and spent evenings in the air-raid shelter under the castle. They were ready to flee at any time and slept in "siren suits", all-in-ones beloved of Winston Churchill.

Prewar, suggestions that Elizabeth might broadcast on the radio were rebuffed. In 1940, the palace changed its mind. Elizabeth gave a speech during *Children's Hour* on the BBC to Britain and North America, aimed at evacuees. As she told them, she and Margaret "feel so much for you, as we know from experience what it means to be away from those we love most of all". It was a propaganda hit in America.

Yet Elizabeth longed for a greater role in the war effort. The King refused. When she turned 16, Elizabeth graduated from the Girl Guides to the Sea Rangers (senior Guides had been known as Rangers since 1920). The Sea Rangers focused on naval training and Elizabeth gained her boating permit and practised dingy sailing — and went on short camps where she had to do the washing-up. In 1945, she was promoted to a Sea Ranger Commodore.

Yet Elizabeth wanted to do more. She begged her father to let her join the services. "I ought to do as other girls of my age do," she said. Finally, the King allowed her to join the Auxiliary Territorial Service in the same year. By this point women had adopted nearly all army driving work.

Elizabeth didn't sleep in the camp dorm in Aldershot. She returned to Windsor each night. However, she worked hard. She had never even held a spanner before, and so, as she said, "everything I learnt was brand new to me — all the oddities of the inside of the car and all the intricacies of map-reading". She later told the politician Barbara Castle that it had been the only time she had been able to test herself against people the same age as her. Photographs of her at work were on the cover of *Time* magazine and every Allied newspaper. She loved her work — and found driving thrilling.

On May 7, 1945, the BBC interrupted a piano recital to announce that the next day would be known as Victory in Europe day. On May 8, the princesses appeared on the balcony of Buckingham Palace, Elizabeth wearing her ATS uniform. That night she and Margaret, with their governesses and some guards, set off to celebrate, dashing incognito through the crowds. As Elizabeth remembered, "all of us were swept along by tides of happiness and relief".

◀ **In the driving seat**
Princess Elizabeth takes the wheel of an ATS ambulance in 1945

▲ **Model princess**
The Sea Ranger princess admires a model boat at the London Sea Scout Exhibition, 1944

▶ **Mother's pride**
The princess during training, under the watchful eye of her mother, Queen Elizabeth, in 1945

▼ **Everyday duties**
Elizabeth happily mucked in with her fellow Sea Rangers. She joined in 1943

▶ **Children's Hour**
Princess Margaret looks on as Princess Elizabeth broadcasts in 1940

▶ **Exciting news**
Princess Elizabeth and Prince Philip at Buckingham Palace on July 10, 1947, after their engagement was announced

▶ **Bridal party**
Princess Elizabeth is driven along The Mall to Westminster Abbey in the Irish State Coach escorted by the Household Cavalry for her wedding to Prince Philip on November 20, 1947

Prince Philip made a lasting impression on the young princess in 1939. Eight years later they were married. By Kate Williams

'How high he can jump!" said Elizabeth to Marion Crawford, in July 1939. The princess and her governess were watching the handsome 18-year-old cadet Prince Philip of Greece leaping over nets on the tennis courts, while her parents made an official visit to the Royal Naval College in Dartmouth. It was 1939, just before the outbreak of the war. Elizabeth was 13 and had lived a sheltered life. Her second cousin once removed, clever, international Philip of Greece was a revelation.

Elizabeth was entranced, much to the delight of Philip's uncle Dickie Mountbatten, who had engineered the meeting. Philip was invited to join the family for tea on the royal yacht, moored near by — and Elizabeth watched, fascinated, as Philip ate a banana

split. When the royal yacht departed Dartmouth, the cadets followed in their little boats — until the King commanded them to turn back. They obeyed — apart from Prince Philip, who rowed hard after them. Elizabeth watched him through her binoculars. Officials shouted at Philip through a megaphone until he finally turned — but the die had been cast.

Philip found the young princess very appealing — cheerful and practical, she was unlike his fragile mother. Philip was born in Corfu, the only son, and fifth and final child, of Prince Andrew of Greece and Denmark and Princess Alice of Battenberg. When Philip was one, a popular uprising forced his uncle King Constantine I of Greece to abdicate and Prince Andrew was exiled from Greece. The family set up in Paris but disintegrated — his mother was put in an asylum and his father took a mistress. Philip was sent to boarding schools and flourished at Gordonstoun in Scotland before going to Dartmouth.

During the war, Philip wrote regularly to Elizabeth and came to stay for Christmas in

1943. With the end of hostilities, he came to court the 19-year-old future queen in earnest. Occasionally they went to concerts or restaurants — at other times they stayed in the nursery with Margaret and drank orangeade.

Elizabeth's circle was not enthusiastic. The King and Queen wished her to "see more of the world" and "meet more men" before marrying. There was concern among courtiers that Philip was not quite the right sort — "no gentleman" — and he signed visitors' books as of "no fixed abode". Elizabeth refused to listen. She had been set on Philip since Dartmouth; the separation of war had only intensified the romance. The King had to relent. The engagement was announced on July 9, 1947, with the wedding fixed for November 20.

The government and courtiers worried that a lavish ceremony might infuriate a population deep in a postwar recession. However, Winston Churchill called it "a flash of colour on the hard road we have to travel" — and his view won. The marriage of the young princess and her handsome prince would be

A PRINCESS IN LOVE

◀ Let us see her!
Police hold back
crowds outside
Buckingham Palace
after the wedding

▲ Royal souvenir
A commemorative
postcard of the
royal wedding

▶ Courting
Elizabeth and
Philip attend
the wedding of
Lady Patricia
Mountbatten,
Philip's first cousin,
in October 1946,
the year before
they became
engaged

◀ Train track
The newly married
couple walk
down the aisle of
Westminster Abbey

▼ In the picture
The couple look
at photographs of
their wedding while
on honeymoon

as magnificent as possible. Yet the day could not be a bank holiday; one day off might plunge the faltering economy into dire straits.

Clothes rationing was still in force and thousands of women donated clothing coupons for the dress — but the palace returned them, because coupons could not be transferred. The Privy Purse found the money for the silk and Norman Hartnell designed the dress, inspired by Botticelli's *Primavera*.

Three thousand presents poured in from all over the world — and half were put on display. Elizabeth received jewels, china, vases, a racehorse, a home cinema, more than 150 pairs of silk stockings, and 500 cans of tinned pineapple from the governor of Queensland. Perhaps the oddest was two pieces of toast — sent by two young women in London who had burnt it in excitement when they heard about the engagement on the wireless.

Two nights before the wedding, the King and Queen held a ball for the royal guests at Buckingham Palace. The King led a conga through the royal apartments. It was a true postwar jamboree. Among those not invited, however, were Philip's three surviving sisters — who were married to German princes. Also staying at home were the Duke and Duchess of Windsor. Neither the princess nor her mother could forgive him for abdicating.

"I can't believe it's really happening," Elizabeth said to her old governess on the morning. At Westminster Abbey, the King escorted his daughter up the aisle, followed by her two five-year-old pageboys, cousins Prince Michael of Kent and Prince William of Gloucester, Princess Margaret and seven other bridesmaids. About 2,000 people were crammed into the stalls — the choir had to sit in the organ loft with the radio commentators.

Elizabeth made her vows and promised to obey her husband — which would be technically impossible when she became Queen.

After the ceremony, 150 guests travelled to Buckingham Palace to dine on partridge casserole (partridges were unrationed) and Bombe Glacée Princess Elizabeth. The cake was created by supplies sent by the Australian Girl Guides, and stood 9ft high and weighed 500lb. While guests dined, news footage was packed up and sent all over the world.

The couple left for their honeymoon first to Hampshire, then Birkhall on the Balmoral estate, through cheering crowds, despite the rain. At the palace, the royal family felt rather deflated. "I can't imagine life without her," said Margaret. Elizabeth had enjoyed the most wonderful day. "I was so happy and enjoying myself so much that I became completely selfish," she wrote to her mother. She hoped that from now on the government would see her as an adult rather than a child.

THE KING IS DEAD

The young Elizabeth left London a princess and flew back a queen. By Valentine Low

Because King George VI died in his sleep it is hard to put an exact time on the moment Princess Elizabeth became Queen. This much is certain, however: she was high up in a fig tree in Kenya, surrounded by wild animals, and did not hear the news until some hours later.

She and Philip were staying at Treetops, a game-viewing lodge in a tree overlooking a waterhole where they could watch the wildlife, on the first leg of a tour that was due to take them to Australia and New Zealand.

On the morning of February 6, 1952, knowing nothing of what had happened at home, they returned to Sagana Lodge,

the farm given to them by the Kenyan government as a wedding present. Eventually Michael Parker, one of the royal party, was told the news over the phone by Martin Charteris, the Queen's private secretary, who was at a hotel a few miles away.

Parker crept around the house to attract Philip's attention and beckoned him out on to the lawn. The news left him utterly shocked.

By the time Charteris found the new Queen, she was at her desk drafting letters of apology for the cancellation of the tour. "What are you going to call yourself?" he asked. "My own name, of course," she replied. "What else?"

On her way back to London she changed from the jeans she had been wearing at Sagana Lodge into the mourning clothes that always travelled with her. Outwardly she was calm, a woman who despite her relative youth — she was 25 — appeared ready for the role that fate had thrust upon her; inside, she was doing her best to conceal the grief she felt at the loss of her father.

On the tarmac at Heathrow, after a 24-hour journey, she was met by Winston Churchill. The prime minister — who was accompanied by the leader of the opposition Clement Attlee; the lord president of the council Lord Woolton; and the foreign secretary

Anthony Eden — seemed so overcome by emotion that he could not speak.

The next day, at St James's Palace, at her formal proclamation as Queen, Elizabeth spoke of "this heavy task that has been laid upon me so early in my life". She said: "My heart is too full for me to say more to you today than that I shall always work, as my father did throughout his reign, to uphold constitutional government and to advance the happiness and prosperity of my peoples, spread as they are all the world over."

It is a promise she has kept for longer, and with a greater devotion to duty, than anyone might have imagined.

> ❝ Asked what she would call herself, she replied: 'My own name, of course. What else?'

◀ A nation mourns
How *The Times* of February 7, 1952, announced the King's death

◀ Shared moment
Princess Elizabeth and the Duke of Edinburgh were at Sagana Lodge in Kenya when they were told of George VI's death

◀ Home to rule
The new Queen is met at Heathrow on February 7 by, *right to left,* Winston Churchill, Clement Attlee, Anthony Eden and Lord Woolton

GETTY IMAGTES; STANLEY DEVON FOR THE TIMES

I VOW TO THEE, MY COUNTRY

The seriousness with which the young Queen took the grandeur and sacredness of the Coronation in 1953 was a sign of her strong sense of duty. But her solemnity was matched by a willingness to listen to her people: she asked for television cameras to film the ceremony at Westminster Abbey, says Valentine Low

▶ **Her majesty**
The official portrait of Queen Elizabeth II, taken by Cecil Beaton after her Coronation

The Queen was only 25 when her father died, while she was on tour in Kenya with Philip, but for all the shock of his death she appeared to be as prepared for her new role as she ever would be. Two days later she was at St James's Palace for the Accession Council, where she made the Accession Declaration and took an oath to preserve the Church of Scotland. One of those present recalled how "a slight figure dressed in deep mourning entered the great room alone, and, with strong but perfectly controlled emotion, went through the exacting task the Constitution prescribed".

The other side of that dedication to duty has always been a tendency to traditionalism, a reluctance to change things unless there is

a good reason to do so. However, that does not mean that the Queen has ever been a stick-in-the-mud, determined to adhere to the old ways at all costs. This was demonstrated early on in the volte-face made by the palace over the question of whether television cameras would be allowed into Westminster Abbey for the Coronation. During the planning the modernisers were keen to have the ceremony televised, while the traditionalists were opposed, arguing that it was essential to preserve the mystique of royalty. It was also felt that there were moments of the ceremony that were so sacred they should remain private. The Queen sided with the traditionalists, as did Winston Churchill, who felt that allowing in

television would put too much strain on the Queen, and an announcement was duly made that television cameras would be banned from the abbey.

There was immediate uproar. The papers demanded, "Let the people see the Queen", and the palace soon beat a hasty retreat. It was the Queen herself, who had originally thought that the cameras would be inappropriate, who decided it was time to listen to the people. As Sarah Bradford wrote in her biography: "When she saw how much her people wanted to see her actually crowned and how outraged they were that they should be excluded from a spectacle confined only to high officials, peers and foreigners, Elizabeth became convinced that the ban

Loyal subjects
The newly crowned Queen, in the Gold State Coach, passes cheering crowds en route from Westminster Abbey to Buckingham Palace

Crowning glory

The Coronation in numbers

- ◆ 8,251 guests attended the ceremony at Westminster Abbey.

- ◆ 129 nations and territories were represented at the service.

- ◆ The officers and men from the armed forces taking part in the procession or lining the route totalled 29,200.

- ◆ The return route to Buckingham Palace was designed so that the Queen could be seen by as many people as possible. The 4.5-mile route took the 16,000 participants two hours to complete. The procession stretched for nearly two miles.

- ◆ There were more than 2,000 journalists and 500 photographers from 92 nations on the route. Thirty cameramen were stationed in the abbey.

was a mistake." The television cameras were allowed into the abbey, but — in a last concession to those wanting to preserve at least some of the magic — not allowed to film the anointing and the communion, the most sacred parts of the service.

For everyone involved, the Coronation was heavy with the weight of symbolism. For the government, still wrestling with postwar austerity, the new Queen represented the nation's fragile hope. It was also an opportunity to promote the cause of the newly established Commonwealth, one that the Queen adopted with equal enthusiasm. When Norman Hartnell was designing her coronation dress, she asked him to embroider it with the symbols of the Commonwealth countries, such as the lotus flower of Ceylon and the wattle of Australia, as well as the traditional British emblems of the English rose, the Scottish thistle and the Welsh leek.

Above all, though, it was a solemn and sacred statement of her pledge to serve her people. After taking the Coronation Oath, in which she promised to govern her peoples — in Britain and overseas — according to their respective laws and customs, and to maintain the "Protestant reformed religion established by law", she moved to the altar and, laying a hand on the Bible, swore: "The things which I have here before promised, I will perform and keep. So help me God."

The Queen kissed the Bible and signed the oath, and then took her place in St Edward's chair, where, under a canopy held unsteadily by four Garter knights, the Archbishop of Canterbury anointed her, saying: "As Solomon was anointed by Zadok the priest and Nathan the prophet, so be thou anointed, blessed and consecrated Queen over the peoples whom the Lord thy God hath given thee to rule and govern."

The seriousness with which the Queen regarded the promises she made that day is the key to how she has governed her life since. The fact that she regards her position not as an honour, or a privilege, or even a calling, but a sacred duty means that she has never shrunk from her commitment to serve.

On a day-to-day basis, that still can be

▲ **Playing to the crowd** The newly crowned Queen waves from the balcony of Buckingham Palace, as Prince Charles, Princess Anne, Prince Philip, the Queen Mother and Princess Margaret look on

▶ **Happy Times** The front page of *The Times* on June 3, 1953

◆ The crown placed on the Queen's head by the Archbishop of Canterbury was the St Edward's Crown, made in 1661. Made of solid gold, it weighs almost 5lb.

◆ The Imperial State Crown, worn by the Queen on her return to the palace, contains four pearls traditionally believed to have been Queen Elizabeth I's earrings.

◆ The Queen appeared with her family on the balcony of the palace still wearing the Imperial State Crown and the Royal Robes to greet the crowds. She appeared again at 9.45pm to turn on the "lights of London". Lights cascaded down The Mall from the palace, lighting the huge cipher on Admiralty Arch and turning the fountains in Trafalgar Square into liquid silver, until floodlights from the National Gallery to the Tower of London had been illuminated.

seen in the attitude she takes to her work. She reads her red boxes without fail, from the latest cabinet minutes to the weekly summaries from her realms across the world. Whether it is the latest Foreign Office correspondence or a briefing from Canada in French (no translation required; the Queen is fluent in French), all are studied and carefully digested. She still keeps her weekly meetings with the prime minister.

"She is very assiduous and careful about reading things and when you discussed things with her, she had read them very carefully," her former deputy private secretary Mary Francis once said. "You don't very often get a question or a comment. But you know it's all sinking in and almost certainly some of it gets played back when she meets the prime minister at her weekly meeting or has her audiences with new ambassadors."

Harold Macmillan, her prime minister at the beginning of the 1960s, wrote in his diary that he was "astonished" at her grasp of detail.

The Queen's dedication to duty is so much part of the fabric of the nation, an aspect of her which people have come to expect without question, that it is often taken for granted even as she reaches the age of 90.

Well into her ninth decade the Queen has been carrying out a solid 400 engagements or so every year. On one notable occasion in 2014, at the end of a state visit to France that included an official ceremony in Normandy to mark the 70th anniversary of the D-Day landings, the Queen undertook a morning of engagements in Paris, only to dash back to Britain by helicopter in time for the Epsom Derby.

In 2015, the year that Elizabeth became the longest reigning monarch in British history, she undertook 341 engagements — 306 in the UK and 35 abroad. Every day she still scans newspapers and reviews her correspondence — 200 to 300 letters a day.

Whether it is conducting the State Opening of Parliament, hosting foreign heads of state, or laying the wreath at the Cenotaph on Remembrance Sunday, the Queen shows an energy and a resilience that would be remarkable in a woman 20 years younger. At 90, she remains our devoted and glorious monarch.

'I RELY ON MY FAITH TO GUIDE ME'

The Queen believes in the power of religion as a force for good and reconciliation, says **Ian Bradley**

Although reserved about what she rightly regards as a personal matter, the Queen has made no secret of her Christian faith. Together with her belief that she was called and anointed by God, it has sustained and strengthened her throughout her reign.

There are very few Sundays when she is not in church, and her regular attendance is a matter of conviction rather than duty. She was, of course, brought up in the Christian faith and schooled in the Victorian virtues of duty, discretion and dignity by her parents. There is some evidence that as a girl she felt that she was at the receiving end of rather too much religious teaching. At the age of ten she is said to have responded when asked by the Archbishop of Canterbury Cosmo Gordon Lang whether she would like to join him in a walk through the Sandringham gardens: "Yes, very much, but please don't tell me anything more about God. I know all about Him already." The next year she wrote an account of her father's Coronation complaining that "at the end the service got rather boring as it was all prayers".

These early protestations aside, Princess Elizabeth soon showed that she had the same strong faith as her father, grandfather and great-great-grandmother. In her first broadcast, made at the age of 14 during the darkest days of the war in October 1940, she spoke directly to children who had been evacuated from their homes, telling them: "God will care for us and give us victory and peace."

It has been in her more recent Christmas Day broadcasts that she has most clearly revealed the strength and nature of her faith. In the first five decades of her reign these were often essentially glorified travelogues. A radically new tone was introduced in the 2000 broadcast when the Queen, speaking directly to camera, made what could only be described as a personal testimony: "For me the teachings of Christ and my own personal accountability before God provide a framework in which I try to lead my life." This particular broadcast attracted 25 times more letters to Buckingham Palace than any previous royal Christmas message.

Encouraged by its reception, the Queen has continued to make frequent allusions to her faith in subsequent Christmas broadcasts. In 2002, reflecting on a year in which she mourned the deaths of her mother and sister and celebrated her Golden Jubilee, she said: "I know just how much I rely on my own faith to guide me through the good times and the bad." In her most recent Christmas Day broadcast, in 2015, she quoted from St John's Gospel — "The light shines in the darkness, and the darkness has not overcome it" — and spoke of her personal identification with this message.

Although rooted in Protestant Christianity, and feeling most at home with its tenets and style of worship, she has reached out warmly and generously to those of other denominations and religious traditions. In her 2004 Christmas broadcast she movingly retold the parable of the Good Samaritan and called for greater understanding and respect between those of different faiths and cultures.

This has been a heartfelt and oft-repeated plea, springing from her belief in the power of religion as a force for good and reconciliation, and in the continuing validity of the teachings of the world's leading faiths.

▼ Called by God
With the Archbishop of Canterbury Rowan Williams in 2012

▲ **Team Windsor** The royal couple celebrate their silver wedding anniversary at Balmoral in 1972

'My strength and stay' A marriage to bind a nation

The Queen's partnership with Prince Philip has underpinned the most beloved monarchy the United Kingdom has known, says Sally Bedell Smith

The indelible image of the Diamond Jubilee weekend in June 2012 was of the Queen and the Duke of Edinburgh standing on the upper deck of the royal barge for nearly four hours in the rain. Aged 86 and 90, enduring chill and blustery winds, they showed fortitude as well as gratitude to the 1.2 million people along the banks of the Thames.

It was everything that symbolises the royal couple. They are tough, stoic, duty-bound, a team. A beacon of continuity throughout decades of change, they have set an example and solidified the traditions that help to bind the nation.

Their mutual devotion radiates a "sense of unqualified commitment that has been so characteristic of every aspect of this reign", said the Archbishop of Canterbury Rowan Williams when they celebrated their 60th wedding anniversary in 2007. Among the places they visited that year

was Malta, where they had enjoyed a carefree existence as a young married couple when Philip was posted with the Royal Navy.

In 2015 they returned to the island nation for a state visit — a sentimental three days that took them back to favourite haunts such as the Marsa racecourse, where Princess Elizabeth had watched her husband play polo. On the first night they attended a reception for Malta's great and good. It had been a long day that included a three-hour flight and welcoming ceremony yet the Queen was animated and engaged as she circulated through the crowd, and Philip left a trail of laughter.

If the Queen is constant and calm, the Duke of Edinburgh is a spritz of vinegar with his irreverent and sometimes caustic comments. However, he has always said "supporting the Queen" is his primary purpose as her consort and he has held true to this

'Cherish Lilibet? I wonder if that word is enough to express what is in me.' [She is] 'the only "thing" in this world which is absolutely real to me and my ambition is to weld the two of us into a new combined existence that will not only be able to withstand the shocks directed at us but will also have a positive existence for the good'

IN A LETTER TO HIS MOTHER-IN-LAW
WHILE ON HONEYMOON, 1947

'He is someone who doesn't take easily to compliments but has, quite simply, been my strength and stay all these years, and I, and his whole family, and this and many other countries, owe him a debt greater than he would ever claim or we shall ever know'

AT HER GOLDEN WEDDING ANNIVERSARY SPEECH AT BANQUETING HOUSE, LONDON, NOVEMBER 1997

◀ **Newlyweds**
Previous page, left: the princess and the duke on their honeymoon at Broadlands, Hampshire, in 1947

◀ **Attention!**
Previous page, right: the Queen gets the

giggles as she passes the Duke of Edinburgh in uniform at Buckingham Palace in 2005

▶ **One for the album**
Top: the Queen takes a photo in Tuvalu, on a tour of the South Pacific in 1982

▶ **In profile**
Middle: one of a series of portraits taken at Buckingham Palace in November 2001 to commemorate the Golden Jubilee the next year

▶ **Sky's the limit**
Bottom: in the Solomon Islands during their 1982 South Pacific tour

for nearly seven extraordinary decades. Her marriage to her "strength and stay" has arguably held the royal family together through the divorces of three of their four children, and the harrowing week after the death of Diana, Princess of Wales. For Britain and the Commonwealth, their remarkable partnership has created the most successful and beloved monarchy in history.

Princess Elizabeth could have chosen from what her friend Lady Glenconner called "a whole battalion of lively young men", English aristocrats with vast landholdings and wealth. Yet at the unlikely age of 13 she fell in love when she first spent an afternoon with 18-year-old Prince Philip of Greece. He was a naval officer in training and a distant cousin also descended from Queen Victoria and Prince Albert. He had very little money but he was strikingly handsome, confident, intelligent, breezy and energetic.

In the ensuing years Princess Elizabeth came to view Philip as a man of ideas and appealing complexity who would be neither easy nor boring but would share her commitment to duty and service. Despite a protective shell formed during a rootless childhood when he was neglected for long periods by his divorced parents, "Philip had a capacity for love which was waiting to be unlocked", said their mutual cousin Patricia Mountbatten. Elizabeth "would not have been a difficult person to love", she added. "She was beautiful, amusing and gay. She was fun to take dancing or to the theatre." Her curly brown hair framed her porcelain complexion, with cheeks that the photographer Cecil Beaton described as "sugar-pink", vivid blue eyes, an ample mouth that widened into a dazzling smile, and an infectious laugh.

They were married on November 20, 1947, and spent their honeymoon at Birkhall, the 18th-century lodge on the Balmoral estate. "Philip is an angel," Princess Elizabeth wrote to her mother, "he is so kind and thoughtful." He in turn wrote to his mother-in-law: "My ambition is to weld the two of us into a new combined existence that will not only be able to withstand the shocks directed at us but will also have a positive existence for the good."

To a remarkable degree, that wish came true. They had only a few years together before she assumed the burdens of the crown at the tender age of 25. Their time in Malta from 1949 to 1951 was the closest Princess Elizabeth came to an ordinary existence — socialising with other officers' wives, going to the hair salon, even carrying her own cash, although shopkeepers noted "she was slow in handling money".

It was Philip who broke the news to his wife in 1952 that her father had died at the age of 56 and

that she was now the Queen. In the beginning Philip was viewed with suspicion by the old-style courtiers surrounding his wife. He was excluded from the substance of the Queen's official life, with no access to the state papers in her daily boxes. Yet he carved out a significant role for himself as a patron of more than 800 charities and advocate for causes from wildlife conservation to youth fitness, even as his wife came to rely on him for advice when making tough decisions.

If her advisers bring a question to her on a matter outside her head-of-state role, she asks them first to find out what Philip thinks. Her approach to problems is to look at the big picture and ask for other options, while Philip drills down and gets to the heart of a problem — what one of her advisers called "a defence staff rigour", with an ability to "pull an idea to bits, find the good parts and the parts that need work". Her advisers know that if her husband is happy with an idea, she probably will be as well. Early on, Philip saw the potential of television for the monarchy. He encouraged the Queen to use it and even tutored her on how to read from an Autocue for her first televised speech in 1957.

On their trips around the United Kingdom and overseas, they perfected a choreography of turns and cues that appeared effortless. He would watch her intently during their walkabouts to see whether she needed any assistance. He would often spot people who couldn't see her — children in particular — and guide them out of the crowd to a better vantage point. When the Queen needs a boost, he is there with a humorous aside: "Don't look so sad, sausage."

❝

On the eve of the Diamond Jubilee an adviser said: 'She still lights up when he walks into the room'

PREVIOUS: TIM GRAHAM/ANWAR HUSSEIN/GETTY IMAGES; PA; ANWAR HUSSEIN/LICHFIELD/TIM GRAHAM/HULTON ARCHIVE/GETTY IMAGES; MIRRORPIX

◀ **High fliers**
Top: on board a private
jet, from the 1969
BBC film *Royal Family*

◀ **In bloom**
Middle: in a greenhouse
at Balmoral, 1972

◀ **Happy birthday**
Bottom: arriving
at St Paul's Cathedral
for a service of
thanksgiving held
in honour of the
Queen's 80th birthday,
June 15, 2006

While Elizabeth and Philip are not physically
demonstrative, they have a deep connection that
intensified after the deaths of her mother and sister
in 2002, when he became "her emotional
touchstone", in the view of one of her senior
advisers. On the eve of her Diamond Jubilee, the
adviser noticed that "she still lights up when he
walks into the room. She becomes softer, lighter,
and happier." During his carriage-driving
competitions she would watch him do the obstacles,
then run back and jump into her Land Rover to
drive the half-mile to the next set of challenges.

Yet they are not, according to their cousin Lady
Pamela Hicks, "sweet old Darby and Joan by any
means. They're both very strong characters."
Sometimes the Queen has gone to unusual lengths
to avoid confrontations with her prickly husband.
Tony Parnell, for 30 years the foreman of her
home at Sandringham, recalled a time when Philip's
dressing room badly needed to be repainted.
"On Her Majesty's instruction," he said, "we had
to match the dirty paintwork so he wouldn't know.
I don't think he ever knew."

The most poignant moment of the Diamond
Jubilee weekend occurred after Philip fell ill
with a bladder infection after the long day on the
water for the Thames River Pageant on the
Sunday. The Queen's walk down the aisle of
St Paul's Cathedral the following Tuesday was
a throat-catching moment — the first time
she had appeared at a significant ceremonial event
without her husband at her side.

Although well into his nineties, he bounced
back, defying the odds after heart and abdominal
surgeries, to accompany the Queen on her rounds
at home and abroad. In April 2014 they flew to
Rome for five hours to meet Pope Francis.
Less than two weeks later Philip was with her again
to host the historic first state visit of an Irish
president to Britain. That June they joined world
leaders in Normandy for the 70th anniversary of
D-Day and afterwards were the toast of Paris as
they wound up a hugely successful state visit. A year
later they were back on the continent for another
official visit, this time to Germany, where the
crowds were rapturous.

Along the way they celebrated their 66th
wedding anniversary in typically low-key
fashion at the London home of the Queen's cousin
Lady Elizabeth Anson. For the dinner, Lady
Elizabeth used solar-powered Queen statuettes to
hold the place cards for the guests, marking
the Queen's seat with a toy bobble-head corgi.
Surrounded by their oldest friends and extended
family, the royal couple, aged 87 and 92, still
laughed like newlyweds.

THE QUEEN AT NINETY

2

QUEEN AND COUNTRY
THE HEAD OF STATE

The Queen and Prince Philip view *Blood Swept Lands and Seas of Red*, an installation of ceramic poppies at the Tower of London that marked the centenary of the outbreak of the First World War. October 16, 2014

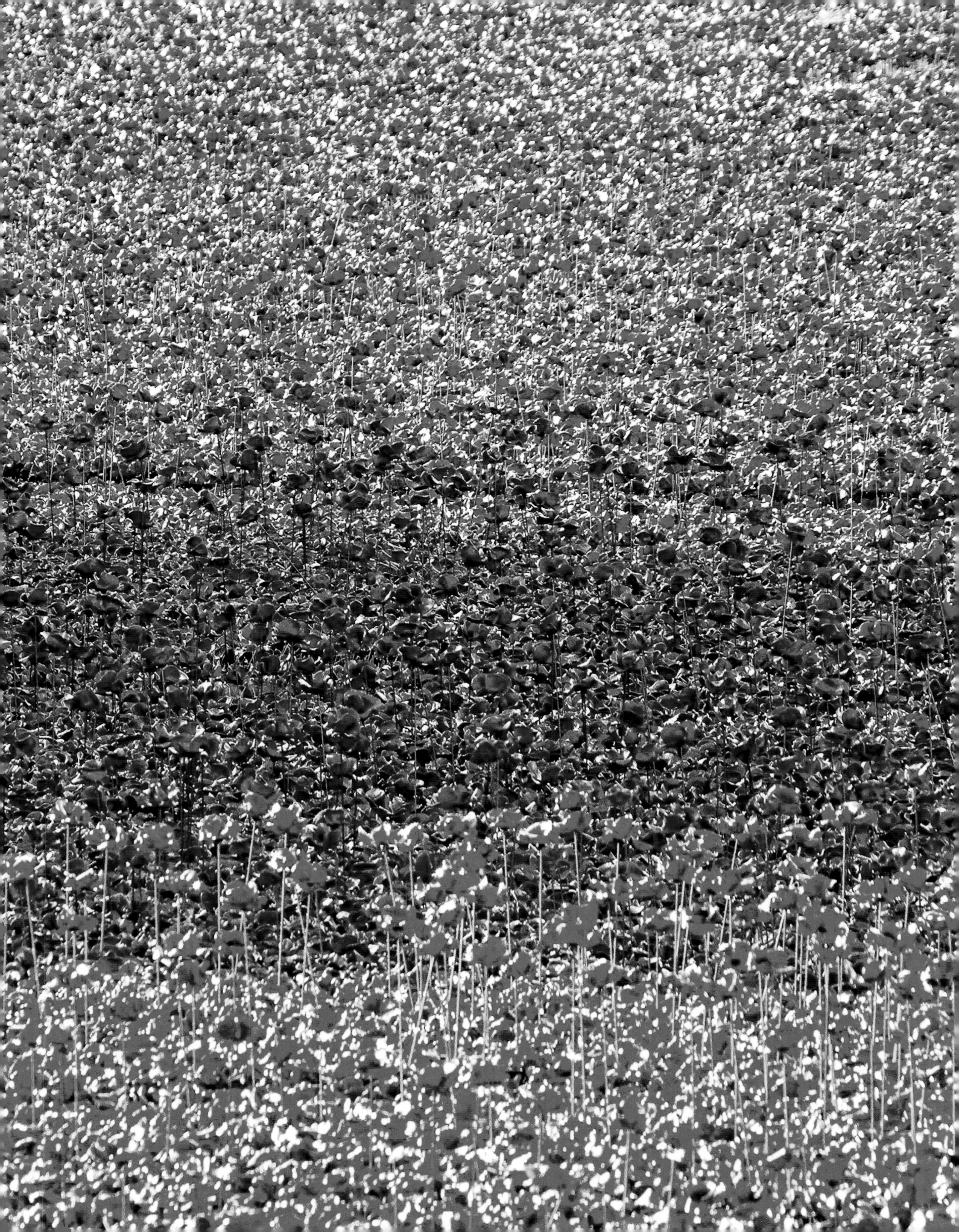

HER MAJESTY'S GOVERNMENT

Twelve prime ministers have served the Queen, travelling to Buckingham Palace once a week for their confidential meetings. They have been as different as the political issues they faced while she remains constant — well prepared, thoughtful and astute, says Valentine Low

Despite the entertaining fantasy promulgated by Peter Morgan in his play *The Audience*, no one really knows what is discussed during the weekly meetings between the Queen and the prime minister. Plenty of people have asked, however. In the early days of her reign, when the Queen was in her twenties and Winston Churchill was more than half a century her senior, his private secretary Jock Colville noticed that as the two of them got to know each other, the meetings got longer and longer. "What do you talk about?" he asked the prime minister. "Oh, mostly racing," he replied.

For all Churchill's jocularity, it would be a mistake to suppose that the meetings were all gossip and small talk. She read her boxes and made sure she always knew what was going on. "The Queen," Edward Heath wrote, "is undoubtedly one of the best-informed people in the world."

Now on her 12th prime minister, the Queen still sees David Cameron — who had not been born when her fifth prime minister, Harold Wilson, came to power — once a week. Inevitably, over the years the Queen has got on better with some of her prime ministers than others, and one suspects that her relationship with Cameron was not improved by his embarrassing indiscretion in revealing how she "purred" down the phone after hearing the result of the Scottish independence referendum.

Churchill adored her and always occupied a special place in her affections; the historian Ben Pimlott in his biography of the Queen described how the weekly meetings would take on an almost jaunty air. "The premier would arrive wearing a frock coat and top hat, with a gleam in his eye, and disappear happily into secret conclave."

Harold Macmillan treated their relationship as what Pimlott called a kind of "chivalrous fantasy", and she got on surprisingly well with Wilson (according to him), despite having little in common with him. He treated her as an equal and aides noted that their audiences grew longer over time. Wilson once described the meetings as the only times when he could have a serious conversation, which would not be leaked, with somebody who wasn't after his job.

Not all of the relationships have been

quite so easy. When Heath first met her, he said: "I lost my nerve and said to her, 'Have you been busy lately, Ma'am?' 'That,' she replied, 'Is the sort of question lord mayors ask when I visit cities.'"

It did not get much better after that. Heath had no small talk and little time for women, and as a member of the household observed, "the Queen found Heath hard going".

Politically too they were at odds: she was a fervent believer in the Commonwealth, while Heath was a passionate European to the exclusion of all else and did not think much of the Commonwealth. In 1971 he wanted her to stay away from the first Commonwealth leaders conference in Singapore because of the expected furious reaction to his plan to resume arms sales to South Africa; it took an intense meeting between monarch and prime minister at Balmoral for her to agree.

Even the most confident and socially adept of prime ministers could be put in their place. Recalling his first audience, Tony Blair said: "She was … direct. 'You are my tenth prime minister. The first was Winston. That was before you were born.' I got a sense of my relative seniority, or lack of it."

The lack of warmth between the Queen and Margaret Thatcher has been well documented, if a little exaggerated. Over time, the Queen grew to respect Thatcher, who was a devoted monarchist; as one of her ministers observed, "no one would curtsy lower than Margaret".

While there may not have been animosity between the two women, there was a lack of mutual understanding. One story has it that the Queen said of her prime minister, in fond mock despair: "Mrs Thatcher never listens to a word I say." Thatcher, in turn, found some of the royal ways baffling, such as the Queen's habit of washing up after Balmoral barbecues with her bare hands. Famously, after one visit she sent her a pair of washing-up gloves.

In 1986, against a background of Thatcher riling some members of the Commonwealth by refusing to back sanctions against South Africa, *The Sunday Times* published a story saying that the Queen was dismayed by some of Thatcher's policies. This went beyond the Commonwealth crisis over South Africa, the paper said: "The Queen considers the prime minister's approach to be uncaring, confrontational and divisive."

The extent to which the Queen believed that is an issue that has long been argued over and not satisfactorily resolved. It is, however, an impression that has not gone away, although the biographer Hugo Vickers has argued that he knows for certain that the Queen was deeply upset by the way Thatcher was ousted in 1990 and immediately gave her the Order of Merit. Whatever their

1

2

differences, there was always a respect between the women. When the Queen attended Thatcher's 80th birthday party as guest of honour, others were touched by the sight of the Queen taking Thatcher's hand as she raised her from a deep curtsy before guiding the frail former prime minister through the throng of assembled friends and admirers.

After Thatcher's death in 2013, the Queen broke with tradition to attend her funeral, the first time since the death of Churchill in 1965 that she had attended the funeral of a former prime minister. That, however, had been a state occasion; this was a personal choice, and one that Thatcher's family said would have left her "humbled".

As the Queen has grown older, and her prime ministers younger, their relationship has changed. When John Major — the first prime minister who was younger than the Queen — succeeded Thatcher, the Queen "discovered in him a more relaxed, congenial visitor than his predecessor", according to Pimlott.

Cameron, whose brother used to go to tea at Windsor because he was at prep school with Prince Edward, revealed how she will occasionally tease him. Although she has not seen *The Audience*, she got wind of the scene in which she supposedly dozes off as Cameron bores her with the latest political

machinations from Europe. Later, the (real) Queen told him that she had never fallen asleep during their weekly meetings. After a dramatic pause, she added: "Yet!"

Of her relationship with Gordon Brown, almost nothing is known. However, he did provide one of the more amusing prime ministerial moments of her reign when he appeared to get lost at a state banquet at Windsor Castle after walking the wrong way round the banqueting table. "Has the prime minister got lost?" the Queen asked. "He disappeared the wrong way at the crucial moment."

While it is certain that the Queen has not shown the slightest inclination to interfere in politics, she found on a number of occasions that it was hard to avoid. During the Suez crisis of 1956 the Queen was in the invidious position of being kept thoroughly informed, thanks to a stream of Foreign Office papers and telegrams, so much so that she knew more of what was happening than a number of ministers, some of whom were notoriously kept in the dark. It also put her in a dilemma with regard to the Commonwealth: did she tell Commonwealth leaders what she had been told in confidence, or did she betray their trust by withholding information that was relevant to their interests?

As for the Queen's position on Anthony Eden's Suez intervention, it seems she was not entirely neutral. "I think the Queen believed Eden was mad," recalled one palace aide. While she may not have gone so far as to protest against the Suez operation, one courtier recalled: "She may have said to Eden something like, 'Are you sure you are being wise?'"

Overseas visits produced their share of dilemmas. In 1961 the Queen had been due to visit Ghana, where the newly independent country was starting to move towards single-party rule and dictatorship. With violence and anti-British feeling on the increase there were valid arguments for cancelling the visit, balanced by fears that to do so would drive Ghana into the arms of the Soviet Union. "She is grateful for concerns about her safety," Macmillan recorded in his diary, "but impatient of the attitude to treat her as a woman."

Determined to support the Commonwealth, the Queen went, and she danced at a state ball with the Ghanaian president. In South Africa a nationalist newspaper complained of "the honoured head of the once mighty British Empire dancing with black natives of pagan Africa"; the Ghanaian press hailed her as "the greatest socialist monarch in the world".

One of the most controversial episodes in the Queen's political life came during the

3

4

5

6

7

REX SHUTTERSTOCK; REBECCA NADEN/PA; PAUL POPPER/ADRIAN DENNIS/AFP/GETTY IMAGES; CHRIS HARRIS FOR THE TIMES

1 An unknown quantity
The Queen with Gordon Brown

2 Major league
John Major was the first prime minister who was younger than the Queen. She found him "more relaxed" than Thatcher

3 Queen's counsel
She is said to believe that Anthony Eden, left, was "mad" for intervening in the Suez crisis and asked him: "Are you sure you are being wise?"

4 Old friends
Fellow Scottish landowner Sir Alec Douglas-Home, pictured with his wife, Elizabeth, would talk about dogs and shooting with the monarch

5 Young pretender
She told Tony Blair, her tenth prime minister: "The first was Winston. That was before you were born"

6 Her Majesty's secret service
Harold Wilson said his audiences with the Queen were his only chance of a serious conversation that would not be leaked

7 On his toes
The Queen is said to have teased David Cameron, here with his wife, Samantha, and the Duke of Edinburgh, that she hadn't fallen asleep in their meetings — yet

► **Her premier premier**
The Queen had a special bond with Winston Churchill, pictured with his predecessor, Clement Attlee, and Attlee's wife, Violet

resignation of Macmillan as prime minister in 1963. He had been thinking — and dithering — about stepping down for some time, and then was forced into action when he had to go into hospital for a prostate operation. This was before the days when the Conservative party elected its leaders; the new leader was supposed to emerge through soundings, although there was no agreed mechanism as to how the process should work.

The ever-devious Macmillan, meanwhile, despite still recovering from his operation, was determined to mastermind the change-over from his hospital bed. Chaos ensued, with the leading contenders jockeying for position, the cabinet divided, backbench MPs throwing in their two ha'p'orth, and Macmillan doing everything in his power to ensure that the obvious candidate — Rab Butler, the deputy prime minister — did not get the job. Buckingham Palace did its best to stay out of the fray, which served only to prompt speculation about what the Queen would do. In the event, Macmillan managed to organise it so that within three quarters of an hour of his eventual resignation the Queen was at his hospital bedside for a farewell meeting. She asked him for his advice, he suggested that she call for Lord Home (who would relinquish his title to become Sir Alec Douglas-Home), and she agreed.

According to Pimlott, the advice was thoroughly unconstitutional, although it may have been what she wanted to hear. An aide told him: "When she got the advice to call Alec she thought, 'Thank God'. She loved Alec — he was an old friend. They talked about dogs and shooting together. They were both Scottish landowners, the same sort of people, like old school friends."

It was, in Pimlott's view, "the biggest political misjudgment of her reign", although other constitutional experts, such as Vernon Bogdanor, disagree. In *The Monarchy and the Constitution* he says she correctly took the most straightforward course and avoided getting involved in the internal politics of the Conservative party.

The controversy caused by the selection process led to a change in the rules of the Tory party and explains why when the Queen faced another constitutionally tricky moment — the 2010 general election, which was widely expected not to produce a party with an overall majority — she ensured that her private secretary had done a thorough job of laying the groundwork with the cabinet secretary so that when the time came for the post-election horse-trading to choose a prime minister, a clearly defined process was agreed and set in place. She was not going to get caught out again.

THE STYLE QUEEN

Dressing the part was not easy at first — there were no role models to follow — but the Queen soon found her own way, says Anna Murphy

'If I wore beige," the Queen once said, "nobody would know who I am." Dressed head to toe in cerise or turquoise, on the other hand, and there is no question as to who One might be, no difficulty in picking One out in a crowd. At heart Her Majesty's sartorial choices are the regal equivalent of the hi-vis jacket, and often almost as bright. (Sunshine yellow has been a favourite shade since the 1980s.)

The Queen has made up her own sartorial rulebook. She has had to; it's not as if there had been a recent precedent for a female British head of state when she succeeded her father in 1952. (And nor will there be a subsequent one; the next three in line to the throne are male.)

Aside from her adherence to colour, she has strong views on hats, for example; above all that she should wear one, but also that the brim should be off the face so as not to inhibit her public getting a clear sightline. She is all about her audience after all.

What else? She likes a two-inch block heel on her shoes (by Anello & Davide) to add height to her 5ft 4in stature without sacrificing comfort. And her boxy patent bags (by Launer) are made with a slightly longer handle so they can be hooked over her forearm without catching on her cuff. Everything she wears, or carries, is custom made; the Queen leaves the high street to the Duchess of Cambridge, thank you very much. No playing the everywoman for her.

The Queen has never seen fashion as a leveller; quite the reverse. Take her 1947 wedding dress, for example. What would be the embattled public's response to her extravagant seed-pearl-and-crystal-encrusted Norman Hartnell confection? Not horror, as some feared, but delight at their twinkly fairytale princess amid all that drear.

It was Hartnell she called on again to make her Coronation dress six years later,

THE BRIGHTS

THE HATS

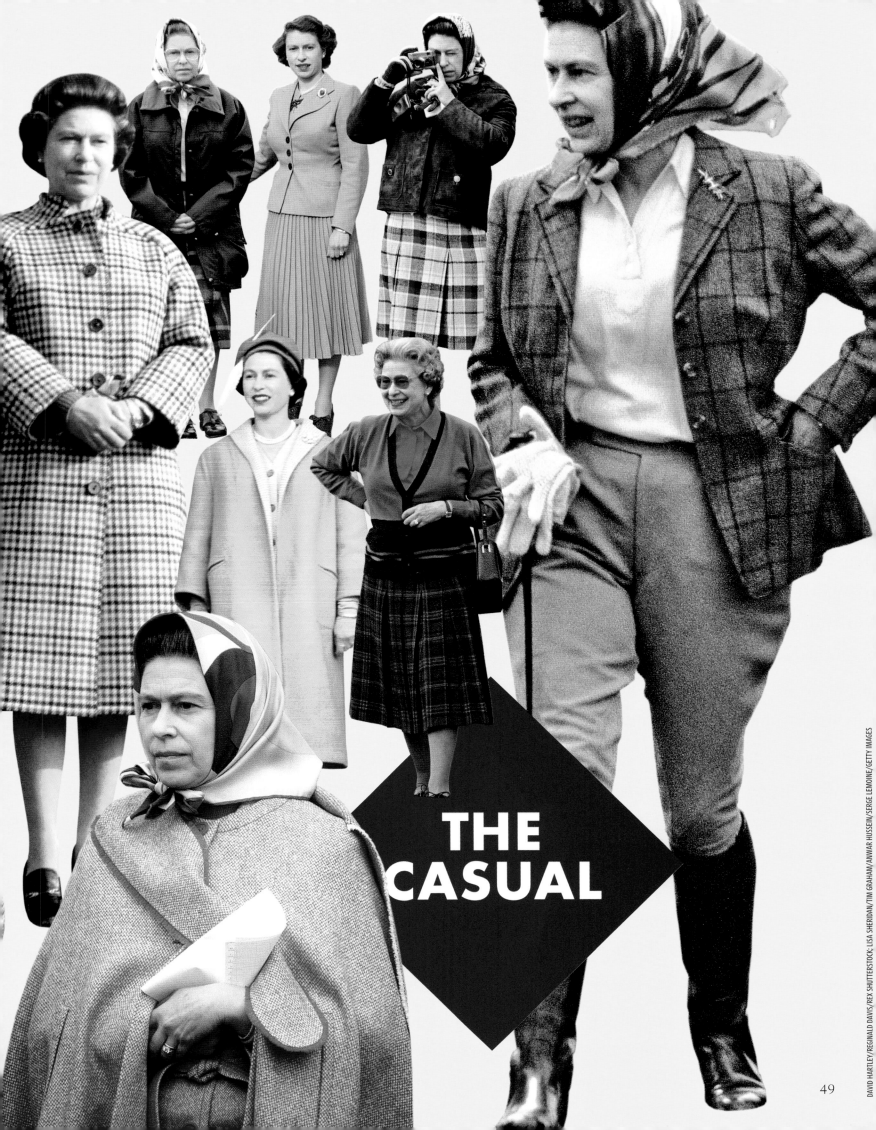

THE CASUAL

insisting that the floral symbols of Great Britain and the Commonwealth be incorporated, from Irish shamrocks to Canadian maple leaves. Those shamrocks reappeared — 2,091 of them this time — embroidered on the robe she wore during her historic 2011 visit to Ireland. On royal tours the Queen has consistently used her clothes to honour her host country.

How could anyone who became monarch the moment a crown was put on her head ignore the semantics of dress? Indeed, so emblematic has the Queen's mode of attire become over the years that you can see its influence on other women in the public eye, from Margaret Thatcher to Hillary Clinton (the former even co-opted those Launer handbags, and loved a hat). We don't only recognise our Queen from her head on our stamps but from her signature ensembles.

Like the good daughter she was, the young Elizabeth used her mother's favourite designer, Norman Hartnell, during early adulthood. However, once she became Queen, she began working with Hartnell to develop a different look, eschewing her mother's fussy school-of-Barbara-Cartland chiffons in favour of sleeker lines. She was a woman in a man's world and she needed to dress to be taken seriously, while still signalling her femininity. She also came to rely upon Hardy Amies, who was celebrated for his subtle retoolings of Parisian trends — think couture with added stiff upper lip. In more recent years the majority of the Queen's wardrobe has been created by Angela Kelly, who has served as her senior dresser since 2002. The daughter of a Liverpool dock worker, Kelly is also the Queen's personal assistant and close confidante.

Away from the public eye the Queen has never needed any help getting dressed. She wears clothes that don't get in the way of walking and riding (dogs and horses respectively): tweed skirts, lace-up brown shoes, sensible woollies, a headscarf, assorted hardcore varieties of raincoat. (She's Queen of the notoriously drizzly British Isles after all.) The colours she chooses are those of our country, her country: earth, moss, heather, lichen. She wears a kind of camouflage. In her private life she can, at last, blend in.

THE GOWNS

▶ **Carriage for two**
With Nelson
Mandela, president
of South Africa, in
1996. Their strong
friendship meant
he was said to have
been one of
the few to be on
first-name terms
with the monarch

DAVID CHESKIN/PA

THE QUIET DIPLOMAT

The Queen is a big hitter on the international stage, using not only her wisdom and experience but also her charm as she discreetly works her magic to win over the most unlikely admirers, says Valentine Low

The Queen fulfils her international role in a way that no British sovereign has done before. From her first triumphant tour as Princess Elizabeth to the delicate diplomacy of the 2015 Chinese state visit, she has met many world leaders, and they have often been highly impressed.

She still works a unique brand of magic. When the Chinese president Xi Jinping visited Britain in October 2015, the palace welcome was treated by China as the sort of affirmation they could get nowhere else in the world. It had been the same in Germany that summer, when Angela Merkel abandoned a meeting on the Greek economy to spend more time with her guest.

Even when she has been among the most stellar players on the international stage, the Queen has shown a quiet magnetism that has remained undiminished — to say nothing of a capacity to surprise. When she and Michelle Obama put their arms around each other at a Buckingham Palace reception, it showed the Queen to be warmer and more affectionate than some have supposed, and less bound by protocol than those who surround her. The bond forged between them paved the way for a successful state visit by President Obama two years later. Some bonds are stronger than others. When Vladimir Putin visited in 2000, he had tea with the Queen at Windsor Castle — a relatively brief visit that did not, presumably, feature any hugs. Three years later the Russian president paid a state visit that was notable, among other things, for his being 15 minutes late for the ceremonial welcome.

One of her warmest relationships was with Nelson Mandela. The South African president is reported to have been one of the few people who got away with calling her Elizabeth; she called him Nelson. They got off to a good start long before he was elected president. Recently released from prison, Mandela had been invited to the 1991 Commonwealth summit in Harare but, because he was not a head of government, he had not been invited to the Queen's banquet. Her courtiers, unsure what to do, asked her. "Let's have him," she said. They got on, it was said, "like a house on fire".

Mandela even got the Queen to behave in unQueen-like ways. On his state visit to Britain in 1996 he asked for a concert at the Royal Albert Hall instead of a banquet. When, during the rousing finale, he got up to dance, she did likewise. "Good heavens," said one establishment figure. "The Queen is dancing!"

In an era when we are accustomed to the international celebrity status of the Duchess of Cambridge, and before her Diana, Princess of Wales, it is easy to forget that the young Elizabeth had a star quality at least as great, if not greater. Crowds came out in their thousands to see her, and statesmen found themselves falling for her charms. In a postwar world short of glamour and fun there was fanciful talk of the "Faerie Princess". Later, when youth and beauty were no longer the most important weapons in her armoury, she employed her wisdom and experience to useful effect. On more than one occasion the British government owed some of its foreign policy successes to the backstage diplomacy carried out unnoticed by the Queen.

She won her first international admirers before she became Queen. As Princess Elizabeth, she undertook a tour of Canada in 1951 that included a trip to the US. President Truman was smitten. Afterwards the British ambassador, Sir Oliver Franks, wrote to the King to say that when Truman appeared with her in public he conveyed "the impression of a very proud uncle presenting his favourite niece to his friends". Truman himself said: "When I was a little boy, I read about a fairy

The Queen with:
1 The Indian prime minister Indira Gandhi, 1983.
2 Zimbabwe's president Robert Mugabe, 1994.
3 The German chancellor Angela Merkel, 2009.
4 President Bill Clinton and his daughter, Chelsea, 2000. **5** President Barack Obama, 2011. **6** US secretary of state Hillary Clinton and the French president Nicolas Sarkozy, 2009. **7** The Polish president Lech Walesa, 1991. **8** The Irish president Michael D Higgins, 2014. **9** President Richard Nixon, Princess Anne and Prince Charles. **10** Pope John Paul II, 1982.
11 President Gerald Ford, 1976.
12 Emperor Hirohito of Japan, 1975. **13** President George W Bush, 2007. **14** Emperor Haile Selassie of Ethiopia, 1954

princess, and there she is." His successor, Dwight Eisenhower, became a firm friend. When the Eisenhowers were guests at Balmoral in 1959 he admired some home-made drop scones and she promised to send him the recipe. Later, she wrote to the president: "Seeing a picture of you in today's newspaper standing in front of a barbecue grilling quail reminded me that I had never sent you the recipe of the drop scones which I promised you at Balmoral. I now hasten to do so and I do hope you will find them successful." She concluded: "I think the mixture needs a great deal of beating while making and shouldn't stand around too long before cooking."

Even the Russians were won over. When Nikita Khrushchev visited Britain in 1956 the Communist party general secretary likened her to "the sort of young woman you'd be likely to meet walking along Gorky Street on a balmy summer afternoon".

When Britain was negotiating to enter what was then called the Common Market, it tried to overcome French objections by inviting General Charles de Gaulle for a state visit in 1960 to charm him into submission. He was given a ceremonial welcome and a state dinner and was delighted that all the royal family came to a banquet at the French embassy. He appreciated the Queen's fluency in French and realised, he wrote, that "she was well informed about everything, that her judgments, on people and events, were as clear-cut as they were thoughtful, that no one was more preoccupied by the cares and problems of our storm-tossed age". Unfortunately, de Gaulle still said "Non".

During her state visit to Morocco in 1980, after erratic behaviour from King Hassan II, including his failure to appear for a luncheon until 5pm, he pointed at Robert Fellowes, her assistant private secretary at the time, and said he was responsible for the "terrible muddle". The Queen rebuked him: "I'll thank you not to speak to my staff like that."

The Queen has had to put up with some fairly unsavoury guests. She was uncomfortable entertaining Nicolae Ceausescu, the Romanian leader, during his state visit in 1978; out walking her dogs in the gardens at Buckingham Palace, she hid behind a bush rather than converse with the dictator and his wife.

She was most angry with President Mobutu of Zaire, who visited in 1973; his wife smuggled a small dog through customs and ordered it steak from the palace kitchens. The deputy master of the household was told: "Get that dog out of my house!" It was duly put on a plane to Brussels.

The Queen's one great advantage over most democratically elected leaders, and certainly all British statesmen, is that she has been around much longer than any of them.

Her longevity proved useful in the Commonwealth crisis of 1979, when African leaders turned against Britain for what they saw as its failure to act against white-ruled Rhodesia. As the former Commonwealth secretary-general Sir Sonny Ramphal said: "Julius Nyerere [of Tanzania] and Kenneth Kaunda [of Zambia] and people like that from Africa were young men when she became Queen, making their way in political life. She knew them as young prime ministers and young presidents and so over many years they were friends."

The Commonwealth heads of government meeting in Lusaka, which Margaret Thatcher initially refused to attend, seemed set to be a disaster. "Britain was looked on with the greatest possible distrust," said a minister. Not the Queen, however; when she arrived the government-owned *Zambia Daily Mail* contrasted her "extraordinary loving heart" with Thatcher's lack of sympathy.

Sir William Heseltine, the Queen's deputy private secretary at the time, said that the Queen helped the foreign secretary, Lord Carrington, to win over Thatcher to his plan to persuade the conference that the Rhodesia question was best solved by Britain, not the Commonwealth. As head of the Commonwealth, the Queen was seen as transcending national boundaries. Kaunda recalled a conversation in Lusaka: "She said, 'My friend, you and I should be careful. We are under the scrutiny of the British prime minister.' I looked up and Mrs Thatcher had her eyes fixed on us." Softened up by the Queen, Kaunda swept Thatcher on to the dancefloor after the opening banquet and the meeting ended with an agreement that led to the negotiations for the peaceful establishment of an independent Zimbabwe.

The Queen was brought into play during the Falklands crisis in 1982. Britain had American support for a military response to the invasion but it was important to strengthen the bond. During a stay at Windsor Castle Reagan found the Queen "charming, down-to-earth", and went riding with her. In a speech to parliament, he confirmed his backing for the UK over the Falklands.

In her eighties the Queen still played an important role. The success of her state visit to the Republic of Ireland in 2011, when she laid a wreath to fallen Irish nationalists, was a triumph of her brand of quiet diplomacy. In 2014 it was followed by a state visit by the Irish president, Michael D Higgins, during which she shook hands with Martin McGuinness at Windsor Castle. The important work was, perhaps, done behind the scenes. However, for many it is those moments in Dublin and Windsor that will go down in history — and the way the Queen, as ever, played her role to perfection.

A royal address
Guests listen to a speech by the Queen in honour of the president of Ireland, Michael D Higgins, at a state banquet in Windsor, on April 8, 2014

The state banquet

A banquet for about 170 people is held on the first night of a state visit. Formal gilt-edged invitations are sent out two months before the event and preparation for the banquet begins several weeks in advance.

The 175ft table is normally arranged in a horseshoe shape, with the Queen and her guest of honour seated at the top table.

The table is covered with linen tablecloths centred using specially made measuring sticks; napkins are folded into a Dutch bonnet shape and each guest is allocated 46cm for their setting.

In total, 1,700 pieces of mismatched baroque, rococo and neo-classic cutlery are placed at each of the 170 table settings.

Crockery is taken from King George IV's 4,000-piece grand service, which takes a team of eight three weeks to unpack and repack.

There are 1,020 glasses — six for each guest for water, champagne for the toast, red wine, white wine, champagne or sweet wine and port.

Footmen use measuring sticks to make sure every chair is the same distance down the table and each glass is the same distance from the table edge.

The table is decorated with more than 100 candles in silver-gilt candelabra, along with displays of seasonal fruit and 23 flower arrangements in silver-gilt centrepieces.

The Queen quality-checks the table, correcting a wonky candle, commenting on any new lighting feature and inspecting all the flower arrangements. She is said to miss nothing.

The royal chef is responsible for devising the menu for a state banquet, which traditionally consists of four courses.

The clerk of the royal cellars and the yeoman of the royal cellars, in conjunction with the head of government hospitality, choose the wine, which is selected to match the food, once the menu has been approved.

On banquet nights, 19 stations are set up around the ballroom, each manned by four staff — a page, footman, under-butler and wine butler. When the food arrives the banquet team — about 100 footmen and pages — are synchronised by a system of "traffic lights": blue for "stand by" and amber for "serve the food".

The end of the banquet is signalled by the arrival of 12 pipers processing round the room, a tradition begun by Queen Victoria, whose fondness for bagpipes led her to employ a full-time piper.

The Queen's wine cellar, situated beneath the state rooms in one of the oldest parts of Buckingham Palace, holds 25,000 bottles.

●●
I was taken with her grace and intelligence and the clever manner in which she discussed public issues, probing me for information and insights without venturing too far into expressing her own political views. Her Majesty impressed me as someone who, but for the circumstance of her birth, might have become a successful politician or diplomat

BILL CLINTON AFTER SITTING NEXT TO THE QUEEN AT A D-DAY COMMEMORATION DINNER IN PORTSMOUTH IN 1994

▶ Rank and file
Inspecting the
troops of the
Queen's Own
Nigeria Regiment,
Royal West African
Frontier Force,
which had been
renamed in her
honour before
her visit in
February 1956

53 COUNTRIES, 91

LANGUAGES, ONE QUEEN

The survival of the Commonwealth, representing two billion people around the world, can be credited to the Queen's sheer force of personality, says Giles Whittell

At most of the Queen's public events this year her subjects will turn out in her honour. At several, however, it will be the Queen who does the honouring, and each time the object of her respect will be the same — the Commonwealth.

No other institution except the monarchy itself bears the stamp of the Queen's personality as clearly as this sprawling collection of mainly English-speaking former colonies. It is not universally admired but in a sense it's her life's work. Its expansion has been her proudest accomplishment on the world stage, and it's no coincidence that most of its 53 member states will be represented at her various birthday celebrations.

They will be present at the national service of thanksgiving in St Paul's Cathedral on June 10. They will be represented when The Mall is given over to a gigantic lunch party two days later. The Commonwealth will be a theme of a Queen's Young Leaders reception at Buckingham Palace because membership is part of what these young people have in common. In March, the Queen honoured the Commonwealth twice in one day at Westminster Abbey and Marlborough House.

The Queen's role as head of the Commonwealth gives the lie to the notion that she is powerless. As leader of a vast group of nations with shared aspirations, she wields impressive power whether she likes it or not.

The Queen used this power most memorably in November 2013 when, for only the second time in her reign, she did not attend the biennial Commonwealth Heads of Government meeting (CHOGM). The meeting took place in Colombo. The Sri Lankan capital was recovering from civil war under condemnation for the deaths of about 100,000 civilian Tamils. Aides said the Queen's

non-appearance was not political. What did not need saying was that she was not going to fly halfway round the world to tarnish the Commonwealth by shaking hands with an alleged mass murderer. The effect for President Rajapaksa of Sri Lanka was devastating. In her place the Queen sent her son, and Prince Charles, in his main speech, avoided all mention of the civil war. He ended with a plaintive appeal to the "family values" that the Commonwealth represented. It was an awkward moment. Charles spoke for himself and his mother, and the subset of Commonwealth countries that successfully espouse democracy.

Overlooked in the fuss was the extraordinary fact that the Commonwealth exists at all; that it has expanded to include not just former British imperial possessions, but parts of Francophone Africa and a former Portuguese colony; and that it is the only international body apart from the United Nations to straddle the rich-poor divide on a global scale. The Commonwealth is loose enough not to break apart when stresses build, but coherent enough to function. It represents two billion people — more than a quarter of the world's population. It promotes democratic ideals even if not all its members practise them.

The Queen has been committed to the notion of a global English-speaking body since she was a young woman. Her first tour of the Commonwealth as Queen started five months after her Coronation, covered 40,000 miles and lasted seven months. For her Silver Jubilee she went farther: 56,000 miles. At 76, she marked her Golden Jubilee with trips to Canada, Australia, New Zealand and Jamaica. With very few exceptions she has attended Commonwealth summits not as an observer but as an exceptionally diligent chairwoman. She has made a point of getting to know other leaders, the better to anticipate their moves and moods. She has given hundreds of gifts and accepted hundreds more, among them a totem pole and a canoe.

Her father, George VI, had not taken the idea of a durable successor to the empire seriously. As Richard Bourne, the former head of the Commonwealth Human Rights Group, puts it, running the Commonwealth "just

Tours of duty
The Queen's visits

Bold denotes Commonwealth

ADEN	Apr 27, 1954	LIBERIA	Nov 23, 1961	CANADA	May 3-4, 1970	NORFOLK ISLAND	Feb 11, 1974		Feb 22-Mar 7, 1977
UGANDA	Apr 28-30, 1954	SIERRA LEONE	Nov 25-Dec 1, 1961	CANADA	Jul 5-15, 1970	NEW HEBRIDES	Feb 15-16, 1974	AUSTRALIA	Mar 7-23, 1977
MALTA	May 3-7, 1954	GAMBIA	Dec 3-5, 1961	CANADA	May 3-12, 1971	SOLOMON ISLANDS		PAPUA NEW GUINEA	
GIBRALTAR	May 10, 1954	CANADA	Jan 30-Feb 1, 1963	TURKEY	Oct 18-25, 1971		Feb 18-21, 1974		Mar 23-26, 1977
NORWAY	Jun 24-26, 1955	FIJI	Feb 2-3, 1963	THAILAND	Feb 10-15, 1972	PAPUA NEW GUINEA		AUSTRALIA	Mar 26-30, 1977
NIGERIA	Jan 28-Feb 16, 1956	NEW ZEALAND	Feb 6-18, 1963	SINGAPORE	Feb 18-20, 1972		Feb 22-27, 1974	CANADA	Oct 14-19, 1977
SWEDEN	Jun 8-10, 1956	AUSTRALIA	Feb 18-Mar 27, 1963	MALAYSIA	Feb 22-26, 28, 1972	AUSTRALIA	Feb 27-28, 1974	BAHAMAS	Oct 19-20, 1977
PORTUGAL	Feb 18-21, 1957	CANADA	Oct 5-13, 1964	BRUNEI	Feb 29, 1972	INDONESIA	Mar 15-22, 1974	BRITISH VIRGIN ISLANDS	
FRANCE	Apr 8-11, 1957	ETHIOPIA	Feb 1-8, 1965	MALAYSIA	Mar 2, 6, 8, 1972	BERMUDA	Feb 16-18, 1975		Oct 26, 1977
DENMARK	May 21-13, 1957	SUDAN	Feb 8-12, 1965	SINGAPORE	Mar 5, 1972	BARBADOS	Feb 18-20, 1975	ANTIGUA	Oct 28, 1977
CANADA	Oct 12-16, 1957	GERMANY	May 18-28, 1965	MALDIVES	Mar 13-14, 1972	BAHAMAS	Feb 20-21, 1975	BARBADOS	Oct 31-Nov 2, 1977
UNITED STATES	Oct 17-21, 1957	CARIBBEAN	Feb 1-Mar 6, 1966	SEYCHELLES	Mar 19-20, 1972	MEXICO	Feb 24-Mar 1, 1975	GERMANY	May 22-26, 1978
NETHERLANDS	Mar 25-27, 1958	BELGIUM	May 9-13, 1966	MAURITIUS	Mar 24-26, 1972	JAMAICA	Apr 26-30, 1975	CANADA	July 26-Aug 6, 1978
CANADA	Jun 18-Aug 1, 1959	CANADA	Jun 29-Jul 5, 1967	KENYA	Mar 26, 1972	HONG KONG	May 4-7, 1975	KUWAIT	Feb 12-14, 1979
INDIA	Jan 21-Feb 1, 1961	MALTA	Nov 14-17, 1967	FRANCE	May 15-19, 1972	JAPAN	May 7-12, 1975	BAHRAIN	Feb 15-17, 1979
PAKISTAN	Feb 1-16, 1961	BRAZIL	Nov 5-11, 1968	YUGOSLAVIA	Oct 17-21, 1972	FINLAND	May 25-28, 1976	SAUDI ARABIA	Feb 17-19, 1979
INDIA	Feb 16-26, 1961	CHILE	Nov 11-18, 1968	CANADA	Jun 25-Jul 5, 1973	USA	Jul 6-11, 1976	QATAR	Feb 21-22, 1979
NEPAL	Feb 26-Mar 1, 1961	AUSTRIA	May 5-10, 1969	CANADA	Jul 31-Aug 4, 1973	CANADA	Jul 13-25, 1976	UAE	Feb 24, 1979
INDIA	Mar 1-2, 1961	CANADA	Mar 2-3, 1970	FIJI	Oct 16-17, 1973	LUXEMBOURG	Nov 8-12, 1976	OMAN	Feb 28-Mar 2, 1979
IRAN	Mar 2-6, 1961	FIJI	Mar 4-5, 1970	AUSTRALIA	Oct 17-22, 1973	WESTERN SAMOA	Feb 10-11, 1977	DENMARK	May 16-19, 1979
ITALY	May 2-5, 1961	TONGA	Mar 7, 1970	CANADA	Jan 27, 1974	TONGA	Feb 14, 1977	TANZANIA	Jul 19-22, 1979
VATICAN CITY	May 5, 1961	NEW ZEALAND	Mar 12-30, 1970	COOK ISLANDS	Jan 28-29, 1974	FIJI	Feb 16-17, 1977	MALAWI	Jul 22-25, 1979
GHANA	Nov 9-20, 1961	AUSTRALIA	Mar 30-May 3, 1970	NEW ZEALAND	Jan 30-Feb 8, 1974	NEW ZEALAND		BOTSWANA	Jul 25-27, 1979

KENYA	Feb 4-6, 1952
BERMUDA	Nov 24-25, 1953
JAMAICA	Nov 25-27, 1953
FIJI	Dec 17-19, 1953
TONGA	Dec 19-20, 1953
NEW ZEALAND	Dec 23, 1953-Jan 30, 1954
AUSTRALIA	Feb 3-Apr 1, 1954
COCOS ISLANDS	Apr 5, 1954
CEYLON	Apr 10-21, 1954

▼ **Feathered friends**
The Queen is greeted
by children dressed
in carnival costumes
in Port of Spain,
Trinidad, in 2009

THE CHANGING COMMONWEALTH

■ **1952**
8 countries

■ **Present
members**
53 countries

*(including countries
from 1952)*

wasn't as much fun as being emperor of India". The King's daughter was more concerned with duty than fun, and understood that the Commonwealth had to be on the right side of history. She had grave misgivings about Anthony Eden's bellicose response to the Suez crisis in 1956 and, according to her assistant private secretary at the time, may have gone as far as to remonstrate with him over his decision to retake the canal by force.

She smoothed the path to Zimbabwe's independence, persuading Zambia's president Kenneth Kaunda to remove a potentially inflammatory reference to Robert Mugabe and Joshua Nkomo as "freedom fighters" from his speech at the Lusaka CHOGM in 1979. She lobbied behind the scenes for democracy and against military dictatorship in Nigeria, and where democracy took root, she did her best to help it flourish. In one case highlighted by historians she was able to prevail on Ghana's charismatic president Jerry Rawlings to stand down at the end of his term (in 2001) rather than follow the disastrous example of Africa's self-appointed presidents-for-life.

Most importantly and courageously, the Queen sided with justice and the Commonwealth against Britain's own Conservatives in the long struggle against South African apartheid. It seems unconscionable now that

Edward Heath defended selling arms to South Africa on the grounds that they would not be used to enforce apartheid and Britain had an inalienable right to set its own trade policies. The Queen thought it unconscionable in 1971. She consented with reluctance to Heath's demand that she should not attend that year's CHOGM in Singapore. The government tried to persuade her not to go to the next meeting either, in Canada, but she went anyway.

The rift between Buckingham Palace and Margaret Thatcher over South African sanctions was deep and enduring. Thatcher's refusal to back the embargo led to a broad boycott of the 1986 Commonwealth Games in a personal humiliation for the Queen. She continued to attend summits even so, including an especially difficult one in Limassol in 1993 when Greek Cypriots branded her a killer for Britain's hanging of nine anti-British rebels nearly four decades earlier.

By the early 1990s the Commonwealth was limping. It had split over South Africa, played no role in ending the Cold War and was sidelined by the Queen's own government as an annoying irrelevance for having the temerity to lecture Britain on its moral shortcomings when its members harboured

ZAMBIA Jul 27–Aug 4, 1979	**JAMAICA** Feb 13-16, 1983	**GRENADA** Oct 31, 1985	**FRANCE** Jun 9-12, 1992	**INDIA** Oct 12-18, 1997	**ESTONIA** Oct 19-20, 2006
SWITZERLAND	**CAYMAN ISLANDS** Feb 16-17, 1983	**TRINIDAD AND TOBAGO**	**CANADA** Jun 30-Jul 2, 1992	**BRUNEI** Sep 17-20, 1998	NETHERLANDS Feb 5, 2007
Apr 29-May 2, 1980	MEXICO Feb 17-22, 1983	Nov 1-3, 1985	GERMANY Oct 19-23, 1992	**MALAYSIA** Sep 20-23, 1998	UNITED STATES May 3-8, 2007
AUSTRALIA May 24-28, 1980	**CANADA** Mar 8-11, 1983	NEPAL Feb 17-21, 1986	HUNGARY May 4-7, 1993	SOUTH KOREA Apr 19-22, 1999	BELGIUM Jul 11-12, 2007
ITALY Oct 14-17, 1980	SWEDEN May 25-28, 1983	**NEW ZEALAND** Feb 22-Mar 2, 1986	**CYPRUS** Oct 18-24, 1993	**GHANA** Nov 7-9, 1999	**MALTA** Nov 20, 2007
VATICAN CITY Oct 17, 1980	**CYPRUS** Nov 9-10, 1983	**AUSTRALIA** Mar 2-13, 1986	**ANGUILLA** Feb 18, 1994	**SOUTH AFRICA** Nov 9-15, 1999	UGANDA Nov 21-24, 2007
TUNISIA Oct 21-23, 1980	KENYA Nov 10-14, 1983	CHINA Oct 12-18, 1986	**DOMINICA** Feb 19, 1994	**MOZAMBIQUE** Nov 15, 1999	TURKEY May 13-16, 2008
ALGERIA Oct 25-27, 1980	**BANGLADESH** Nov 14-17, 1983	**HONG KONG** Oct 21-23, 1986	**GUYANA** Feb 19-22, 1994	**AUSTRALIA** Mar 17-Apr 2000	SLOVENIA Oct 21-22, 2008
MOROCCO Oct 27-30, 1980	**INDIA** Nov 17-26, 1983	**CANADA** Oct 9-24, 1987	**BELIZE** Feb 22-24, 1994	**ITALY** Oct 16-19, 2000	SLOVAKIA Oct 23-24, 2008
NORWAY May 5-8, 1981	**CYPRUS** Mar 25-26, 1984	**AUSTRALIA** Apr 19-May 10, 1988	**CAYMAN ISLANDS** Feb 26-27, 1994	NORWAY May 30-Jun 1, 2001	**BERMUDA** Nov 24-26, 2009
AUSTRALIA Sep 26-Oct 12, 1981	JORDAN Mar 26-30, 1984	SPAIN Oct 17-21, 1988	**JAMAICA** Mar 1-3, 1994	**JAMAICA** Feb 18-20, 2002	**TRINIDAD AND TOBAGO**
NEW ZEALAND Oct 12-20, 1981	**CANADA** Sep 24-Oct 7, 1984	**BARBADOS** Mar 8-11, 1989	**BAHAMAS** Mar 6-8, 1994	**NEW ZEALAND** Feb 22-27, 2002	Nov 26-28, 2009
SRI LANKA Oct 21-25, 1981	PORTUGAL Mar 25-29, 1985	**SINGAPORE** Oct 9-11, 1989	**BERMUDA** Mar 8-10, 1994	**AUSTRALIA** Feb 27-Mar 3, 2002	**CANADA** Jun 28-Jul 6, 2010
CANADA Apr 15-18, 1982	**BELIZE** Oct 9-11, 1985	**MALAYSIA** Oct 14-17, 1989	**CANADA** Aug 13-22, 1994	**CANADA** Oct 4-15, 2002	UNITED STATES Jul 6, 2010
AUSTRALIA Oct 5-13, 1982	**ST KITTS AND NEVIS**	**NEW ZEALAND** Feb 1-16, 1990	RUSSIA Oct 17-20, 1994	**NIGERIA** Dec 3-6, 2003	UAE Nov 24-25, 2010
PAPUA NEW GUINEA	Oct 23, 1985	ICELAND Jun 25-27, 1990	SOUTH AFRICA Mar 19-25, 1995	FRANCE Apr 5-7, 2004	OMAN Nov 25-28, 2010
Oct 13-14, 1982	ANTIGUA Oct 24, 1985	**CANADA** Jun 27-Jul 1, 1990	**NEW ZEALAND**	GERMANY Nov 2-4, 2004	IRELAND May 17-20, 2011
SOLOMON ISLANDS Oct 18, 1982	**DOMINICA** Oct 25, 1985	UNITED STATES May 14-17, 1991	Oct 30-Nov 11, 1995	**CANADA** May 17-25, 2005	**AUSTRALIA** Oct 19-29, 2011
NAURU Oct 21, 1982	**ST LUCIA** Oct 26, 1985	KENYA Oct 7, 1991	POLAND Mar 25-27, 1996	**MALTA** Nov 23-26, 2005	ITALY Apr 3, 2014
KIRIBATI Oct 23, 1982	**ST VINCENT AND**	NAMIBIA Oct 8-10, 1991	CZECH REPUBLIC Mar 27-29, 1996	**AUSTRALIA** Mar 11-16, 2006	VATICAN CITY Apr 3, 2014
TUVALU Oct 26-27, 1982	**THE GRENADINES** Oct 27, 1985	ZIMBABWE Oct 10-15, 1991	THAILAND Oct 28-Nov 1, 1996	**SINGAPORE** Mar 16-18, 2006	FRANCE Jun 5-7, 2014
FIJI Oct 30-Nov 1, 1982	**BARBADOS** Oct 28-29, 1985	**AUSTRALIA** Feb 18-25, 1992	**CANADA** Jun 23-Jul 2, 1997	LITHUANIA Oct 16-17, 2006	GERMANY Jun 23-26, 2015
BERMUDA Feb 13, 1983		**MALTA** May 8-10, 1992	**PAKISTAN** Oct 6-12, 1997	LATVIA Oct 18-19, 2006	**MALTA** Nov 26-28, 2015

◄ **Air of Mustique**
Princess Margaret, who had a house on Mustique, welcomes the Queen to the Caribbean island during her Silver Jubilee tour, 1977

▲ **Deck dance**
The Queen and Prince Philip are entertained by Fijian traditional dancers on board the Royal Yacht Britannia, 1977

▼ **Cuddly friends**
Visiting a wildlife park in Brisbane during her hugely successful tour of Australia in 2011

▼ Great eastern
At the Taj Mahal in Agra during a visit to India in 1961 and, below, admiring the fashions

▶ Mango, Ma'am
Touring a market in the British Virgin Islands, 1977

plenty of their own. Yet it survived. More than that, it thrived. Over the next 20 years South Africa rejoined after a 33-year suspension, and non-Anglophone developing countries started to apply for membership. For Cameroon and Mozambique it was granted in 1995; for Rwanda in 2009.

A 2011 report by the preposterously named Eminent Persons Group said the Commonwealth was drifting from its reformist mission and was hypocritical over human rights. Undaunted, the Queen urged it to dust itself down, respond to new challenges such as food insecurity and climate change, and "stay fit and fresh for tomorrow".

The same year, the Commonwealth had a long moment in the sun on the Queen's triumphant 11-day tour of Australia that took in Canberra, Brisbane and Melbourne. She opened that year's CHOGM in Perth, observing that such meetings' importance "has always been in precise relationship to their relevance". It was a neat, disarming touch. The theme of the summit was "women as agents of change" and she urged all to continue to strive together to promote the theme in a lasting way.

The Queen had been met at the start of the tour by Australia's first woman prime minister. Julia Gillard, an avowed Republican, had refused to curtsy and bowed awkwardly on the red carpet instead. Aides said the Queen "couldn't give two hoots". She swept all before her on her 16th visit to a country that has always reciprocated her affection. Before departing, she and Prince Philip were guests at a barbecue on Perth's Esplanade, attended by about 200,000 people.

Four years later, aged 89, the Queen resumed her role of leading the Commonwealth from the front. After the Colombo hiatus she took Prince Philip with her to host the heads of government in Malta. The trip was partly down memory lane, to a villa she had lived in before ascending the throne. But it was also the fulfilment of a duty to the Commonwealth she said she still cherished after more than 60 years.

The Commonwealth remains a popular and useful global forum — popular for the 5,000 athletes who competed in the 2014 Commonwealth Games in Glasgow; useful for advocates such as Malala Yousafzai, shot in the head while going to school in Pakistan. The guest of honour at the 2014 Commonwealth Day service in London, Malala embodies the Commonwealth's ideals as well as the Queen herself.

Kaunda once remarked that the transition from empire to Commonwealth was made possible by the Queen's personality. "Without that," he said, "many of us would have left."

REGAL TIMES

On February 28, 1985, the Queen visited The Times to watch the production of the newspaper in its 200th

No monarch had ever before attended our morning conferences. The then editor, Charles Douglas-Home, nephew of a prime minister and cousin of the soon-to-be Princess of Wales, was the least likely man to be overawed. But he was cancer-stricken, with less than a year to live, and the unforeseen farce of the day was a severe test of his strength.

Office redecoration was the first sign of trouble. "I hope that the paint line at the end of the corridor does not mean that the monarch will miss Business News," the business editor asked with a hostile smile.

Those on the receiving line had to produce a 20-word biography. The editor was amazed at the lengths to which they would go for a few more. "Do not, in any circumstances, cut the bit about my beagling," said the arts editor. "It's a shared interest, you know."

After her arrival the Queen's first surprise was that our star columnist, Bernard Levin, whom she knew, was part of the same riff-raff line as the rest of us. The cartoonist, Barry Fantoni, had next to explain a joke about homosexuality and *Doctor Who*. "Well, don't make the Dalek too gay," was his instruction. The duke reacted crossly to a story about civil servants leaking documents.

In the newsroom we were attempting the impression of an "active and real" office. The editor had friendly words for the BBC reporters who had been invited to show the best side of *The Times* in its 200th year. He then watched the Queen speak to the comfortingly patrician political and saleroom correspondents before spending several minutes with our Labour editor, Paul Routledge. I was a few feet away with nothing to do but watch what happened next: how two three-letter words become a rumour, how a rumour became a story.

The two words were "one" and "man". The Queen and the Labour editor had been discussing the battle between Mrs Thatcher and the mineworkers' union. According to the whispers, the Queen had said that the strike was "all down to one man and very sad". This "one man" was the Labour editor's friend, Arthur Scargill. Different royal quotations spread through the room.

Just before 1pm we slumped in front of the editor's television. "Our news" came before "the news". The Queen's "unprecedented attack" on Scargill was the gaffe of her reign. A swift call to the palace found a team of courtiers not even bothering to listen.

The editor moved painfully into action. It was "agreed" that there had been a "severe" distinction between what the Queen had said and how the reporters had interpreted her. "Half-heard" became the official phrase. When the royal party returned to see the presses in the evening, the Queen cheerfully asked one of many underemployed print-union workers what he was doing. The duke suggested the crossword.

The rumours only gradually ceased. The duke's leader-conference comment on two officials accused of leaking government secrets had been: "What do you do with s***s like that?" By the evening two different *Times* journalists had told me that the duke had described a *Times* leader as "a load of s***".

I never did find out whether the arts editor had been able to discuss with Her Majesty their "shared interest" in beagling. *Sir Peter Stothard was the editor of The Times from 1992 to 2002. This recollection is adapted from his memoir Alexandria: The Last Nights of Cleopatra, published by Granta in 2013*

▲ **Morning conference**
The Queen, with Rupert Murdoch and Prince Philip to her left, listens in as the editor Charles Douglas-Home, at the head of the table, chairs a meeting with staff. In the left foreground, with beard, is the cartoonist Peter Brookes. Peter Stothard, then features editor, is third from left

BILL WARHURST FOR THE TIMES

▲ **What's news?**
The Queen with
Rupert Murdoch,
proprietor of
The Times, during
an editorial meeting

▲ **Type setting**
Martin Sumner
explains the
processing of
the newspaper

▶ **Page proofs**
Top right: the
Queen listens to
Michael Crozier,
head of special
reports. Editor
Charles Douglas-
Home looks on

▶ **Making the headlines**
How the paper
reported the news
of the Queen's
visit to *The Times*
offices the next day

▲ **Tomorrow's news today**
The Queen sees the
first editions of the
newspaper, ready
for distribution

3

FAMILY AFFAIR
MOTHER, SISTER, GRANDMOTHER

In the first colour photograph of Princess Anne, taken in 1951, Princess Elizabeth holds her baby daughter, while Prince Philip carries Prince Charles

Combining motherhood with her duties as monarch was not always an easy balance to achieve for the young Queen, but underneath her sometimes distant demeanour was a woman who loved her children dearly and juggled her schedule to be there for bedtime, says Sally Bedell Smith

YOUR MAJESTY, MUMMY

LISA SHERIDAN/TIM GRAHAM/GETTY IMAGES

▲ **Sealed with a kiss**
The Queen and Prince Charles share an affectionate moment at a polo match

◀ **Multi-tasking**
The new Queen, Princess Anne and Prince Charles at Balmoral in 1952

When she became Queen at the age of 25, Elizabeth was already the mother of three-year-old Prince Charles and 18-month-old Princess Anne. Her one maternal adjustment to her father's routine was to change the time for the weekly audience with the prime minister from 5.30pm to 6.30pm, which allowed her to join her children in the nursery for their nightly bath and bedtime.

Thus began a lifetime of combining service to her country with her role as a parent, every bit of it under a scrutinising, often critical public eye. Like any mother, she

has had her share of missteps, dramas and rifts with her children. Like all children, they have turned out not quite as she might have expected or planned. Yet if one moment sums up Elizabeth's legacy as a mother and the reciprocal love of her children, it was during the Diamond Jubilee concert in 2012 when Charles addressed her in front of 18,000 people on a grandstand outside Buckingham Palace, and a further half a million watching on large screens in St James's Park, The Mall and Hyde Park. "Your Majesty, Mummy," he said, drawing an unusually huge public smile from her, and great cheers from the crowd.

Then he thanked her "for inspiring us with your selfless duty and service, and for making us proud to be British".

From the outset of her reign, Elizabeth felt it essential to demonstrate her gravitas to the older men who advised her. As a career woman, she was an anomaly in her generation and in the British upper class, combining the roles of monarch, wife and mother without any ready role model. She waited ten years before having her third child, Prince Andrew, and four years later Prince Edward was born, in 1964.

"Nothing, but nothing, deflected her from

duty," recalled Sir Edward Ford, an assistant private secretary to the Queen. "She'd go into labour and have a baby, so we knew we weren't going to see her for a while. But within a very short time, 24 or 48 hours at most, she'd be asking whether there were any papers and would we care to send them up?" She took overseas trips as well; her first extensive tour of Commonwealth countries in 1953 and 1954 kept her away from Charles and Anne for nearly six months.

Her children were fortunate to have a nurturing nanny in Mabel Anderson, who was only a year younger than the Queen and had an affectionate and flexible nature as well as a firm sense of right and wrong. Their maternal grandmother, the Queen Mother, was also an important force who particularly doted on Prince Charles, sometimes to the point of cosseting. Clarissa Eden, the wife of the prime minister Anthony Eden, the first Earl of Avon, was perplexed that the Queen and Queen Mother failed to discipline six-year-old Charles during a picnic at Windsor Castle when he refused to yield his chair to the prime minister. Lady Avon was surprised the Queen "didn't say, 'Come on, Charles, get up,' but I suppose she doesn't like scenes at all cost".

All her children knew that she spent long hours in her office at Buckingham Palace, where her priorities were, as Prince Andrew put it, "work and responsibilities and duties". While the Queen certainly loved her children, she fell into professional habits that pulled her away from motherhood. As a result, she missed out on many maternal challenges as well as pleasures. "She let things go," said Gay Charteris, the wife of the Queen's longtime private secretary Sir Martin Charteris. "She did have work every day. It was easier to go back to that than children having tantrums. She always had the excuse of the red boxes."

"She was not a hugger," said her first cousin Lady Mary Clayton. "She has a different nature. There is a self-containment." The Queen was more visibly engaged with her second set of children. When Mabel Anderson took time off, the Queen felt

relaxed enough to stay in the nursery with Andrew and Edward, tying on an apron for their baths and lulling them to sleep. During weekends at Windsor Castle, the boys zoomed down the gilded Grand Corridor in their pedal cars, and if they fell off their bicycles on one of the gravel paths in the park, the Queen would "pick them up and say, 'Don't be so silly. There's nothing wrong with you. Go and wash off,' just like any parent," Prince Andrew recalled. At teatime, she joined them to watch the BBC's *Grandstand* sports programme on Saturdays and the Sunday cricket league.

All four children found common ground with both parents during their holidays at the family's rural estates, Sandringham in Norfolk and Balmoral in Aberdeenshire. The Queen and Prince Philip taught their children to appreciate their natural surroundings and instructed them how to shoot as well as how to cast into the pools of the River Dee and catch salmon with a well-tied fly. They stalked stag with their parents at Balmoral, and they spent hours on horseback across what Anne remembered as the "miles of stubble fields around Sandringham" and among "the autumn colours of the rowans and silver birches, the majesties of the old Scots pines" at Balmoral. It was perhaps here, away from the pressures of duty, that the Queen was able to bond best with her children, where she was most able to be herself. In more recent decades, the Queen has cultivated a love of country pursuits in her grandchildren too. By the time they were teenagers, Prince William and Prince Harry were regulars on the Scottish grouse moors and at Sandringham for pheasant shoots. Edward, the Earl of Wessex, is a keen shot and attends shoots at Sandringham with his son James, aged eight.

The press of her duties prompted the Queen to make Philip the ultimate arbiter in decisions about their children. She believed his role as head of the family was "the natural state of things". He enforced discipline, and he selected their children's schools, which in the case of Charles reflected Philip's belief in the merit of his own experience rather than what was appropriate for his diffident, sensitive and

awkward eldest son. Charles hated Gordonstoun, the boarding school in Scotland that he found severe, although his younger brothers fared better, not least because by then the atmosphere was more humane with the inclusion of girls. Princess Anne, whose self-confidence and assertiveness mirrored her father's personality, did well at Benenden, her boarding school in Kent.

Particularly with her two eldest children, the Queen believed in the necessity of exposing them to challenging situations and talking to them "on level grown-up terms". "I remember the patience Prince Charles showed when he was around all those adults," said Mary Wilson, the wife of the Labour prime minister Harold Wilson. The royal children may have grown up in a bubble, but the Queen wanted them to work through difficulties and learn to think for themselves.

"I learnt the way a monkey learns — by watching its parents," Charles once said. During Anne's trip to New Zealand with her parents in 1970, the "walkabout" was introduced into the royal routine, a casual stroll to chat and shake hands with ordinary people. "At 19 years old suddenly being dropped in the middle of the street," Anne recalled. "Suddenly being told to pick someone and talk to them. Fun? No, I don't think so."

Anne had a strong bond with her mother through horses, especially when she became a top competitor in the arduous equestrian sport of three-day eventing. Not surprisingly, she was married at a young age, in 1973, to Captain Mark Phillips, an accomplished horseman who won an Olympic gold medal.

The Queen's laissez-faire attitude led to unfortunate consequences when her children reached adulthood, giving her more than her share of heartache. The Countess of Leicester, a neighbour in Norfolk and one of the Queen's ladies-in-waiting, recalled a time when they were writing letters together under an awning at Sandringham. "Suddenly from the bushes to the left there were screams and giggles," the countess later told her daughter Lady Glenconner. "Around the corner came Andrew dragging the gardener's daughter, her

◄ **Working mother**
The Queen salutes
with two-day-old
Prince Edward
in her arms and
four-year-old
Prince Andrew next
to her on the palace
balcony during
Trooping the
Colour in 1964

▶ **View from
the bridge**
In the grounds of
the palace with
Prince Philip,
Princess Anne and
Prince Charles, 1957

◀ **Maternal majesty**
The Queen with her new son, Prince Andrew, 1960

▶ **Family stroll**
Prince Philip, Prince Edward, the Queen, Prince Andrew, Princess Anne and Prince Charles in the grounds of Frogmore on the Windsor estate in 1968

dress in disarray. The Queen took no notice and kept on dictating the letters."

Andrew distinguished himself as a helicopter pilot who saw combat during the Falklands conflict in 1982. On his return after more than five months away, the Queen appeared to wipe tears from her eyes during the flag-waving homecoming at Portsmouth, as her second son greeted her with a red rose between his teeth. She was genuinely pleased in 1986 when he married Sarah Ferguson, a robust and jolly girl who shared the monarch's love of riding and other country pursuits.

Edward, who had his mother's shy streak, struggled after earning his degree at Cambridge. He first bailed out of training as a Royal Marine and then stumbled in trying to establish himself as a film producer. He finally found his footing when he teamed up with his father in running the Duke of Edinburgh's awards for young people. Edward's much later marriage, at age 35, to Sophie Rhys-Jones, a middle-class public relations consultant, drew him closer to his mother. "Sophie first of all respects her as the Queen, then as a mother-in-law, but she also understands that she is a human being and treats her that way," said the Queen's cousin Lady Elizabeth Anson.

Throughout his life, the Queen has "allowed Prince Charles to work at his interests, his aims and his ambitions," said Sir Malcolm Ross, one of her senior advisers. "It is not a cosy relationship," said the Queen's cousin Margaret Rhodes. "They love each other, but the family is not set up to be cosy."

The absence of cosiness made her children's marital break-ups much more difficult for the Queen to recognise and understand, especially with Charles and Diana, Princess of Wales. "I think it took a long time to accept that the faults were not more his than hers," said Patricia Mountbatten, her third cousin. In 1992 — what the Queen called her "annus horribilis" — when Anne, Charles and Andrew split from their spouses, she found it all "nonplussing", recalled Mountbatten. "You don't know how to behave when someone is making such a mess. You want to help them mend, but how to do it?"

The publication in 1994 of Prince Charles's officially sanctioned biography drove a wedge between the heir and his parents. The author Jonathan Dimbleby quoted his complaints that the Queen had been remote during his unhappy childhood and that Philip had been overbearing and insensitive. His parents were wounded and his three siblings were indignant and rebuked Charles to his face. A decade later, after another book that elaborated on these themes, Princess Anne countered that "it just beggars belief" to suggest that her mother was aloof and uncaring, adding that she and her brothers "understood what the limitations were in time and the responsibilities placed on her". Anne said they all appreciated being "allowed to find our own way … People have to make their own mistakes. I think she's always accepted that."

The Queen has steered the monarchy steadily across the decades, reinforcing its place as the linchpin of her country's identity even as she moved subtly with the times. More fundamentally, however, she presides over a modern and effective royal family, despite the hiccups along the way.

After nearly two decades of turbulence, her children have settled down, found happiness in their private lives, and work hard to earn the admiration and affection of the people. With their visible commitment to public service and fulfilment of their royal duties, it is clear that their mother trained them well, instilling in them the values and traditions essential to the institution she still so brilliantly leads.

Sally Bedell Smith is the author of a forthcoming biography of Prince Charles to be published by Random House

◀ **At the wheel**
Driving in Windsor
with Prince Charles
and Princess Anne
in the passenger
seats in 1957,
to the delight of
onlookers

▲ **Fun and Games**
With Prince
Charles, Prince
Edward and Prince
Andrew at the
Montreal Olympics,
July 1976

▲ **Marching orders**
Explaining the
finer points of
Trooping the
Colour to Prince
Edward at
Buckingham
Palace, c 1972

▲ **Expert advice**
At the 1968 Eridge
Horse Trials
in East Sussex,
where Princess
Anne was
competing

▲ **Hero's return**
Meeting Prince
Andrew on his
return from the
Falklands conflict,
where he served as
a helicopter pilot,
September 17, 1982

THE ROYAL TRIUMVIRATE

Until their deaths, the Queen's sister, Margaret, and
her mother were her closest confidantes, a source of fun,
opinion and often worry, says Hugo Vickers

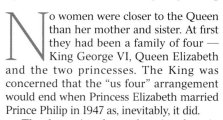

▲ Girls'
best friends
Princess Margaret
and Princess
Elizabeth playing
with the
family dogs

No women were closer to the Queen than her mother and sister. At first they had been a family of four — King George VI, Queen Elizabeth and the two princesses. The King was concerned that the "us four" arrangement would end when Princess Elizabeth married Prince Philip in 1947 as, inevitably, it did.

The dynamics changed again when, in 1952, the King died. The Queen Mother had been virtually acting head of state while the King had been gravely ill. Now she was to change from being a supporting wife to leading life on her own terms — a mixture of the diplomatic, ambassadorial and social.

Throughout her life, however, she remained a quiet force behind the Queen. They talked regularly on the telephone, they went to church at weekends in Windsor, she stayed in the castle for Ascot week and spent time with her at Sandringham. The Queen deferred to her mother in many ways on private family occasions, for example, giving her the King's seat in the chapel at Royal Lodge for Sunday matins. She always allowed her mother a BAE 146 to travel in if she needed it, while this privilege was not automatically granted to Princess Margaret or other members of the royal family. She did not rein in her mother's perceived extravagances, the Queen Mother believing that she should continue to occupy four residences — Clarence House, Royal Lodge, Birkhall and the privately owned Castle of Mey in Thurso were where she entertained extensively.

The Queen continued to run royal life much as in her father's day, out of respect for his memory and to please her mother. Inevitably changes had to be gradually introduced. It was always hinted that the royal family might give up Sandringham but that the Queen Mother would never have approved.

As the Queen Mother reached extreme old age, there is no doubt that she caused the Queen considerable worry by refusing to slow down. The Queen bought her a buggy, decorated in racing colours, but for some years the Queen Mother refused to use it. At the end of a ball to celebrate her golden wedding in 1997, the Queen was heard to say: "I'm trying to persuade Mummy to go to bed." The Queen Mother was 97 at the time. While the public looked on admiringly as the Queen Mother walked the length of the aisle of St Paul's Cathedral at the age of 100, the Queen was anxious that her mother might fall in public.

The death of the Queen Mother at the age of 101, while the cause of sorrow and reflection, also relieved the Queen of considerable stress. As she undertook her Golden Jubilee engagements, she looked more relaxed, began to dress more stylishly, and in a sense asserted her personality in a new way. For many years the Queen Mother had drawn the affection of the nation to her by her outgoing and generous personality. Only in 2002 did the Queen finally, albeit quietly, assume the role of royal matriarch.

The Queen was also very close to Princess Margaret and was frequently concerned about her sister's happiness. They had spent their childhood together, been inseparable during the war and only slightly distanced by the Queen's marriage in 1947. Margaret

Whitlam, the wife of the Australian prime minister, Gough Whitlam, stayed at Windsor Castle in April 1973 and captured something of the relationship between the Queen and Princess Margaret: "You would have loved the sight of the sisters sitting side by side on the deep-piled cream sheepskin rug we gave Her Majesty for her birthday. They looked like 'the Little Princesses' on either one's teenage birthday." She also recorded that the Queen and her sister indulged in proficient imitations — "gentle send-ups" — of people around them, including the Queen Mother.

There were many occasions on which the Queen's public position as monarch clashed with her private feelings. As early as 1953 there was the question of Princess Margaret marrying a divorced equerry, Group Captain Peter Townsend, a man much liked by the Queen and by the Queen Mother. The Queen's private hopes for her sister's happiness were thrown into conflict with her role as head of the Church of England, which at that time was sternly hostile to divorce. Princess Margaret did not have her

▲ **Power of three**
The Queen Mother
— top left, with
Princess Margaret
and the Queen —
refused to slow
down in her old age

▲ **Sister act**
The Queen
celebrates the
Queen Mother's
80th birthday with
Princess Margaret
on August 4, 1980

mother's resilience. Whereas the Queen Mother never disappointed the British public, Princess Margaret was more capricious. She did not aim to please and win over people in the way the Queen Mother did. The royal family were surprised when Princess Margaret married Antony Armstrong-Jones, a photographer, in 1960. The marriage was happy at first but ultimately unravelled. Their separation in 1976 and divorce in 1978 was a time of great sadness and upheaval in Princess Margaret's life and she received the Queen's moral support. In the mid-1990s Princess Margaret's life settled on to a more even keel with the marriages of her children and the arrival of grandchildren, but then her health broke down.

Devoted as the Queen was to her mother and sister, their deaths, within a few weeks of each other in 2002, released her from pressure and anxiety. Inevitably, she minded Princess Margaret's death more. She had been the companion of her childhood, four years younger, and she missed a forceful, animated and spirited person.

FIRE, SEPARATION, TAX — A TRUE ANNUS HÓRRIBILIS

Windsor Castle caught fire, people demanded that the Queen pay tax, and three of her children's marriages failed. Valentine Low looks at how the events of 1992 changed the monarchy

On November 24, 1992, the Queen had a heavy cold. It had been exacerbated by the smoke from the fire that devastated Windsor Castle and it gave added poignancy to a speech she made at Guildhall marking her 40 years on the throne. "Nineteen ninety-two is not a year on which I shall look back with undiluted pleasure," she said. "In the words of one of my more sympathetic correspondents, it has turned out to be an annus horribilis."

It had, indeed, been a terrible year for the royal family: as well as the fire, the marriages of the Queen's three eldest children were all in the process of collapse. Perhaps more importantly the speech marked a turning point in the royal family's relationship with the British people. Bleak in both content and delivery, with its talk of how no institution could expect to be free from scrutiny, the speech was either an appeal for forbearance and understanding or an act of penitence.

It was also a heavy hint of what was to come only two days later. In the Commons, John Major, the prime minister, announced that the following year the Queen and the Prince of Wales would start paying tax on their private income, and that £900,000 of Civil List payments to other members of the royal family would come to an end.

Of the three marriage breakdowns, at least the Queen knew one was coming: the divorce of Princess Anne and Mark Phillips

was finalised in April. The tabloids were rarely short of tittle-tattle from the other two. In January, photographs were published of the Duchess of York on holiday with her Texan friend Steve Wyatt. Six days later the Duke and Duchess decided to separate.

The Prince and Princess of Wales, meanwhile, were conducting a highly public marital war. However, nothing prepared people for the shock of the serialisation in *The Sunday Times* in June of Andrew Morton's book *Diana: Her True Story*. Readers learnt how Diana had deliberately thrown herself down the stairs at Sandringham, and had even slashed her wrists with a razor blade. Her bulimia and depression were charted in devastating detail. While Diana was portrayed as vulnerable and unable to cope, Charles was castigated for his lack of understanding and his relationship with Camilla Parker Bowles.

The Queen was both furious and deeply troubled by it all. In her biography of the Queen, Sarah Bradford painted a vivid picture of the awkward atmosphere at Royal Ascot that year, with Prince Philip refusing to talk to Diana and the Queen in "a pretty bad temper", according to one of her guests.

The scandals kept on coming. In August, the *Daily Mirror* published a picture of the Duchess of York topless by a pool as her friend and so-called financial adviser, John Bryan, kissed her toes. *The Sun* published the transcript of a telephone conversation

between Diana and James Gilbey, in which he called her "Squidgy" and she described her marriage as "torture". Another recording surfaced in November, courtesy of *The Sun*. This time it was the Prince of Wales and Camilla Parker Bowles, and featured the prince uttering such toe-curling endearments as "Your great achievement is to love me."

Discontent about the royals' tax affairs rumbled on. Behind the scenes, moves were already afoot to address the tax question. In public, however, it looked as if the royal family was on the back foot, with both Labour and Tory MPs calling for reform.

Then, on November 20, fire broke out at Windsor Castle after a restorer's lamp set a curtain alight. St George's Hall suffered extensive damage, along with the state dining room and three drawing rooms. Although there was sympathy for the royals, in a woeful misreading of the public mood, the heritage secretary Peter Brooke announced that as the castle was uninsured, the government would foot the repair bill, estimated at £20 million-£40 million. The restoration was later paid for without any recourse to public funds.

On December 9 came the announcement of the separation of the Prince and Princess of Wales. Days later, *The Sun* published the text of the Queen's Christmas broadcast before it went out. The Queen successfully sued for breach of copyright. It would take time before the royal family's standing recovered.

AN UNEASY RELATIONSHIP

Diana's unpredictable nature was a mystery to the pragmatic Queen, says Valentine Low

In one of the most memorable, if not exactly subtle, scenes in the 2006 film *The Queen*, after the death of Diana, Princess of Wales, Helen Mirren comes face to face with a magnificent lone deer that, after a long stare, she shoos away in an attempt to save its life.

Whether this captured the Queen's view of Diana is questionable; after all, it was Diana's brother, Charles Spencer, who called her the most hunted person of the modern age. While sympathetic, the Queen also thought her daughter-in-law behaved badly; she never understood her.

It has always been her attitude not to try to cause trouble, a tendency that showed itself when Prince Charles was considering marrying Diana. While the Queen Mother was strongly in favour, the Queen, according to Charles's biographer Jonathan Dimbleby, "characteristically ... refrained from tendering her opinion".

While Charles and the palace machine never really knew what to do with Diana, the Queen was never less than supportive. The problem, perhaps, was that she was never anything more than supportive either. Diana revered the Queen but the aura that surrounded her, together with the Queen's natural reserve, meant that they never achieved anything like intimacy.

As early as her honeymoon, Diana had the capacity to leave the Queen baffled. At Balmoral, when she had a fit of sulks and refused to come down to dinner, the Queen was mystified as to how someone could behave so badly. While the Queen is said to have liked the glamour Diana brought to the monarchy, it gave her daughter-in-law a power she quickly learnt to use. As relations with Charles went from bad to worse the Queen found herself increasingly torn over how to react.

Diana recounted how whenever the subject of her marriage came up, the Queen would look worried and twiddle her glasses in her hands. Later, according to her lover James Hewitt, Diana summed up the courage to have a frank discussion with her mother-in-law about her problems. "The Queen promised she would do what she could to take some pressure off her, and newspaper editors were asked not to subject her to too much scrutiny," said Hewitt. "But when it came to the issue of marriage to Charles, the Queen said there was nothing she could do. It would be wrong to intervene."

The Queen did her best to remain neutral: whatever Diana had done, she and Philip also disapproved of Charles's infidelity. However, when the Queen wrote to say that divorce was in the country's best interests, Diana was furious.

The Queen's failure to understand Diana became, after her death, a failure to understand the nation's grief. She stayed in Balmoral, thinking it was best for her grandsons; the people thought otherwise. Nearly a week later, she briefly appeared in The Mall to look at flowers and later addressed the country. Speaking "as your Queen and as a grandmother", she called Diana "an exceptional and gifted human being" and said there were "lessons to be drawn from her life and from the extraordinary and moving reaction to her death".

he in-laws
na, Princess
Vales, and
Queen at the
te Opening of
liament in 1982

▲ **Staying neutral**
The Queen preferred not to intervene in Charles and Diana's troubled marriage

▲ **Sea of grief**
The Duke of Edinburgh and the Queen survey the floral tributes to Diana on The Mall

EYEVINE; REX SHUTTERSTOCK; CAMERA PRESS

FAMILY AFFAIR

To the world she is the Queen, but to her eight grandchildren she is "Granny". The Duke of Cambridge once explained the reality of growing up as a grandson of the most famous woman in the world. "She's my grandmother to me first and then she's the Queen."

This was demonstrated most clearly in the hours after the death of his mother, Diana, Princess of Wales, in 1997. The Queen was widely criticised when she did not return from Balmoral to London where large crowds were mourning. On this occasion, however, her instincts as a grandmother trumped her sense of duty as Queen. Her first priority was to stay with William and Harry in Scotland and help them grieve in private.

Long before then William had developed a close bond with his grandmother, whose weekend home was a short walk from his school. Most weekends during his years at Eton College he would walk across the river to spend time at Windsor Castle with "Granny". He and Harry both shouted, "Go, Granny!" during the opening ceremony of the 2012 Olympics when a stunt appeared to show Her Majesty parachuting out of a helicopter with Daniel Craig's James Bond.

After his wedding in 2011, Prince William offered a fascinating insight into how the Queen could cut through royal pomp to ensure he and his intended bride were not swamped by tradition. Once William had announced his engagement to Kate Middleton, palace bureaucracy swung into action on a scale that alarmed the prince. "I was given this official list of 777 names — dignitaries, governors, all sorts of people — and not one person I knew," he recalled. "They said: 'These are the people we should invite.' I looked at it in absolute horror and said: 'I think we should start again.' I rang [the Queen] up the next day and said: 'Do we need to be doing this?' And she said: 'No. Start with your friends first and then go from there.' And she told me to bin the list. She made the point that there are certain times when you have to strike the right balance. And it's advice like that which is really key, when you know that she's seen and done it before."

The Queen's grandchildren are Prince William and Prince Harry, sons of the Prince of Wales; Princess Beatrice and Princess Eugenie, the daughters of the Duke of York;

TO HER EIGHT GRANDCHILDREN SHE'S SIMPLY GRANNY

The Queen had to juggle motherhood with being a new monarch, so no wonder she relishes being a grandparent, says *Damian Whitworth*

▶ **Generation game**
From left:
Peter Phillips,
Zara Tindall,
Prince Harry and
Prince William

Peter Phillips and Zara Tindall, the children of the Princess Royal; Lady Louise Windsor and James, Viscount Severn, the offspring of the Earl of Wessex.

She also has five great-grandchildren: Prince George and Princess Charlotte, Savannah and Isla Phillips, and Mia Tindall.

The Queen particularly enjoys her annual pre-Christmas lunch at Buckingham Palace, which provides an opportunity to get as much of the extended family together as possible.

The Queen is also known as "Granny" to Prince George. That became clear after Charlotte's christening, when William was heard telling him, "we can go back to Granny's". That would be Sandringham, the main house on the estate where they also live, in Anmer Hall.

The Duke of York once suggested that the Queen had been more comfortable as a grandmother than she had been a mother, which was hardly surprising given that she was a young woman when she had to juggle motherhood with monarchy.

"She's been a fantastic grandmother to Beatrice and Eugenie and probably revels in that more than being a mother, to some extent. Always interested and concerned for what the girls are up to," Prince Andrew said at the time of her Diamond Jubilee.

Eugenie describes a grandmother who "lights up" around her grandchildren. She would take them raspberry picking when she was young and listened to Eugenie's stories of life at Newcastle University, taking an interest in what essays she was writing.

In recent years the Queen has been very close to her youngest grandchildren, the children of the Earl of Wessex, who decided against giving them the titles of prince and princess. The family live at Bagshot Park, a short drive from Windsor, where the children often go riding with their grandmother.

As a young girl, Lady Louise, now 12, bore a striking physical resemblance to her grandmother at the same age and spends time talking horses with the Queen at the Royal Mews at Windsor, where her pony is stabled.

The Queen likes nothing more than to attend events where she has a role as both grandmother and Queen. At William's passing-out parade at Sandhurst in 2006 she managed to make her grandson smile

◀ **A great granny**
The Queen "lights up" around her grandchildren, according to Prince Andrew's daughter Princess Eugenie

▼ **Young blood**
From left: Princess Beatrice, Princess Eugenie, Lady Louise Windsor and James, Viscount Severn

" She combines all her
virtues as a leader
and as a head of
state with those of
being a wonderful,
caring grandmother
— to whom we, her
grandchildren, are
utterly devoted

PRINCE HARRY, 2012

" [She is] truly one of the
most amazing women
ever. She is also very
funny ... All I can say is
that she has this air of
magic about her

PRINCESS EUGENIE, 2008

as she inspected the solemn-faced new officers in her role as commander-in-chief of the armed forces. William said that his grandmother likes to laugh about things that have gone wrong at formal events. "The Queen has seen so many parades or performances, when there's a small slip-up it tickles her humour."

He also says, however, that for a grandson who will one day sit on the throne, she is a constant source of counsel.

"There's no question you can ask, and no point you can raise, that she won't already know about — and have a better opinion about," he told the author Robert Hardman for his book *Our Queen*. "And for me particularly, being the young bloke coming through, being able to talk to my grandmother, ask her

questions and know that there's sound advice coming back is very reassuring."

After going to see victims of the Australian floods and New Zealand earthquake in 2011 William received a note from the Queen congratulating him on the way he represented her. "When you get a letter from her or a bit of praise, it goes a long, long way, more so than anyone else saying, 'Well done!' to you. There's such gravitas behind those words."

She has seen her grandchildren make mistakes, but their indiscretions come with the added complication that they were often splashed across newspapers: Harry in a Nazi uniform, smoking cannabis or playing strip poker in Las Vegas; William landing his helicopter in the back garden of Kate's parents' home. One of the few occasions when

Buckingham Palace made it clear that the monarch disapproved of a grandchild's behaviour was when Peter Phillips sold the photographs of his wedding at Windsor Castle to *Hello!* magazine. And there were raised eyebrows when his sister, Zara, and her husband, Mike Tindall, appeared in the same magazine with Mia.

There is no doubt that in private the Queen can be clear and forthright when she needs to be. William may have found Granny was relaxed about the wedding guest list but when he started weighing up which military uniform he would wear on the day, she told him there was no question he should wear his Irish Guards uniform. "I was given a categorical, 'No, you'll wear this!' So you don't always get what you want, put it that way."

▲ **Horsing around**
James, Viscount
Severn, and
Lady Louise
Windsor, seen in
2011, often ride with
their grandmother
at Windsor Castle

GEORGE AND CHARLOTTE

In the Duke and Duchess of Cambridge's children, the future is secure, says Valentine Low

It is a close call as to which has the greater power to increase the popularity of the monarchy: a royal wedding or a royal birth. However, there was no doubt that the arrival of Prince George in July 2013 was yet another boost for the royal family's public standing. Even the most curmudgeonly republicans silenced their complaints for a day.

Prince George was more than just a bonny baby, however. His birth heralded something far more important: it signified lineage and longevity. The point was brought home in fairly unsubtle style at George's christening in October of that year when an official photograph was released showing, for the first time since 1894, four generations of the royal family gathered together: the Queen, the Prince of Wales, the Duke of Cambridge and Prince George. The line of succession was, barring some terrible misfortune, safe for many decades to come.

The Queen, of course, was delighted at the birth of the third in line to the throne (her third great-grandchild). Two days after George was born, she took the rare step of driving to Kensington Palace to meet the new addition. Usually, visitors come to see her.

Prince George was an immediate international superstar. He was inundated with presents from all over the world, and he accompanied his parents to Australia and New Zealand the following year. At home, he has been a regular visitor to Buckingham Palace, where the duchess started taking him for weekly swimming lessons before he turned one — a habit that will have strengthened his relationship with his great-grandmother. He even went there on his first birthday, the same day that the Queen made a point of attending his birthday party at Kensington Palace. If the birth of Princess

Charlotte in May 2015 — in and out of the Lindo Wing at St Mary's Hospital in a day — was surrounded by marginally less excitement, as the line of succession had been secured, there was still plenty of fanfare, from gun salutes to the equally traditional vigil outside the hospital by foreign news crews.

By then, the Cambridges had moved into Anmer Hall on the Sandringham Estate, which can only have pleased the Queen, allowing her the opportunity to see George and Charlotte more frequently, and with far less public scrutiny, than she does in London.

Fantastic four
The Duke and Duchess of Cambridge released this photograph in 2015 to celebrate their first Christmas as a family of four

Little sister
Prince George peers into Princess Charlotte's pram after her christening last year

JELF / AFP / GETTY IMAGES; MATT DUNHAM/PA

4

ROYAL LIFE
THE EVERYDAY
MONARCH

The Queen looks towards
Balmoral during the royal family's
annual summer holiday in
September 1971. The photograph
was taken as part of a series
for use during the Queen and
Prince Philip's silver wedding
celebrations in 1972

THE QUEEN AT HOME

Whether at Buckingham Palace, Windsor Castle, Balmoral or Sandringham, the Queen
prefers relatively simple pleasures and the outdoor life. Shows of extravagance are saved
for state visits, says Hugo Vickers

At state banquets the gold plate comes out. The Queen has been known to point out to state visitors that she does not live like that every day. In contrast, the Queen lives simply, even if on the outskirts of considerable grandeur. She enjoys pleasures such as walking and feeding her dogs, and riding in the grounds at Windsor, Sandringham and Balmoral. Unlike Queen Elizabeth the Queen Mother, she is not personally extravagant.

She divides her time between four royal residences: Buckingham Palace, her official residence and what can be considered the monarch's main office; Windsor Castle, where she weekends in the Victorian Tower overlooking acres of garden, distant fields and woodland; Sandringham, the sprawling Edwardian mansion that is the place for Christmas and where the stud is based; and Balmoral, her gothic Victorian Scottish residence, the place for summers in the Highlands — and for the August weekend visit from the prime minister and his wife.

At the palace, the Queen and the Duke of Edinburgh occupy a long corridor on the Constitution Hill side of the building. The place has the feel of a rather grand Edwardian hotel. The duke, whose rooms once belonged to King George VI, has a library, a large drawing room, a smaller study, his bedroom and a bathroom. Beyond lie the Queen's rooms, which were formerly used by her mother: an audience room, where she receives formal visitors in some style, followed by her dining room where she dines if she doesn't have an official engagement, a study sitting room (with a bow window), bedroom and dressing room. When the Queen is in her rooms, a page stands outside the door.

We have occasional glimpses of the Queen in her private surroundings when she records her Christmas broadcast to the Commonwealth. Her rooms are formal and grand with fine furniture and paintings, and on every table there are photographs of her children, grandchildren and great-grandchildren, alongside signed photographs of foreign monarchs, many of them cousins. She has a private entrance into the garden, where footmen can be spotted walking the corgis, when she cannot do that herself. She can also emerge from her rooms into the state rooms along the garden side of the palace,

through a mirror door, which swings open so she is suddenly there.

At Windsor Castle the Queen's private apartments, where she can make her own breakfast, overlook the Long Walk. She likes to ride her pony and walk her dogs in the Home Park. The Countess of Wessex and her children often ride with her. On Sundays she drives herself to morning service in the Royal Chapel at Royal Lodge and sometimes goes for post-matins drinks with Margaret Rhodes, her cousin, or to another home in the park, such as the deputy ranger's.

At Easter, there is the Easter Court, when the Queen stays at the castle for about three weeks. Guests — often the heads of charities or leading lights in their field — are invited to what is known as a "dine and sleep". They are shown to their rooms where their suitcases are unpacked. The Queen and the Duke of Edinburgh preside at a dinner party and afterwards there is often a tour of the royal library, where items will have been brought out, according to their interests. They say goodbye at the end of the evening. They don't see her again the next morning and they leave after breakfast.

The Queen spends the week after her official birthday in June at Windsor and, after entertaining the Knights and Ladies of the Garter on the Monday, she spends five days at Royal Ascot. Although this has a formal side with a carriage procession, she does not consider it a public duty: it is a pleasure. As such, it is perhaps the only occasion when, to some extent, she politely ignores other racegoers. Her interest is the horses.

For the Christmas break and occasionally in the summer she goes to Sandringham. Here the atmosphere is similar to many country houses owned by the aristocracy — life is directed towards the outdoors.

The Queen takes her summer holiday at Balmoral between July and October. Local landowners are invited to dinner and there is a succession of house guests — mainly family friends and relatives.

The Queen drives visitors around the estate in her Land Rover, or treats them to the traditional royal family "cook out". The duke conducts proceedings on a specially designed barbecue, which travels in a trailer behind a Land Rover, with food and drink in compartments. It means that the royal family can

▶ **En famille**
The Queen and
Prince Philip with
their children at
Sandringham in
1969, from
left: Edward,
Anne, Charles
and Andrew

▶ **Clad in plaid**
When at Balmoral
the Queen usually
wears tartan

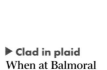

dispense with staff; the Queen likes to do the washing-up herself on these occasions.

The prime minister and his wife are invited for a night at Balmoral at the end of August. This tends to coincide with the Braemar Games on the Saturday and a visit to Crathie church on the Sunday, at which the prime minister might read a lesson. A key event is the private audience with the Queen in her informal sitting room. Other than that, the visiting PM is expected to merge into the royal family's life, accompanying the Queen on a stroll around the kitchen garden, or perhaps visiting the Prince of Wales at Birkhall.

Entertaining prime ministers is a variable feast for the Queen, with stories that have become the stuff of legend. Mrs Thatcher apparently tried to take over the washing-up after a barbecue. The Queen Mother happened to see Tony Blair and his wife arrive one year. Cherie was reluctant to curtsy, and the Queen Mother was heard to say: "Stiff knees, stiff knees." On the other hand, Gordon Brown was a more easygoing guest than his public persona would suggest.

▶ **Emerald Queen**
On the sofa with a
corgi in 1969 in a
still taken by Joan
Williams during the
making of the BBC
film *Royal Family*

THE QUEEN AT NINETY

12 BALMORAL

9 SANDRINGHAM

16 CASTLE OF MEY

17 HIGHGROVE

Balmoral 14
12 ✦ 13
12
✦ 15
✦ 16

9 10
11 Sandringham
Windsor
18 5 2 1
Highgrove ✦ 8 ✦ 3 London
17 7 6 4

THE ROYAL RESIDENCES

Hugo Vickers

LONDON

1. Buckingham Palace
(owned by the nation) Open to the public July to October
Built as Buckingham House for the 1st Earl of Arlington in 1677. Enlarged for John, Duke of Buckingham, between 1702 and 1705. Since Queen Victoria's reign, it has been the official residence of the monarch. The Queen and the Duke of Edinburgh moved there reluctantly in 1952 on Winston Churchill's insistence. It has 19 state rooms, 57 royal and guest bedrooms, 188 staff bedrooms and about 92 offices.

2. Clarence House
(owned by the nation) Open to the public in August
The official residence of the Prince of Wales, it is attached to St James's Palace and shares its large garden. Built

by John Nash between 1825 and 1828 for the Duke of Clarence (later William IV). The Queen lived there as a newlywed. The Queen Mother lived there from 1953 until 2001. After her death, Prince Charles took it over.

3. St James's Palace
(owned by the nation)
Built between 1532 and 1540 for Henry VIII. The last monarch to live there was William IV. Prince Charles moved there after separating from Diana, Princess of Wales, in 1992. The Princess Royal and Princess Beatrice and Princess Eugenie have apartments there.

4. Kensington Palace
(owned by the nation) State apartments open to the public
Bought by William III and Mary II in 1689 and later

improved by Christopher Wren and Nicholas Hawksmoor. The Prince and Princess of Wales lived there after their marriage in 1981 and Diana continued to live there after their separation. Today, the Duke and Duchess of Cambridge live in Princess Margaret's former apartment 1A. Prince Harry lives in Nottingham Cottage in the grounds. Also home to the Duke and Duchess of Gloucester, the Duke and Duchess of Kent, and Prince and Princess Michael of Kent.

WINDSOR
5. Windsor Castle
(owned by the nation) Open to the public most days
William the Conqueror built a fortress on the site in 1066 and it has been a home to most English monarchs

since. When the Queen came to the throne she made it her weekend home. State banquets are held in St George's Hall.

6. Royal Lodge
(owned by The Crown Estate)
Home of the Duke of York. Set in Windsor Great Park, it was given to the Queen's parents in 1931. The Queen Mother used it as her weekend home. She died there in 2002.

7. Frogmore House
(owned by The Crown Estate) Open to the public occasionally
Built in about 1680 in the Home Park, half a mile from the castle by the Royal Burial Ground. It now houses a royal museum. Lunches and dinners are held here, mainly by the Duke of Edinburgh and the Earl of Wessex.

8. Bagshot Park
(owned by The Crown Estate)
Home of the Earl and Countess of Wessex, 11 miles from Windsor Castle. Built as a lodge for Charles I, it was rebuilt in 1879 for Queen Victoria's third son, the Duke of Connaught. Contains a billiard room constructed by Indian craftsmen.

NORFOLK
9. Sandringham House
(privately owned by the Queen) Partly open to the public when the Queen is not in residence
The traditional location for the royal family Christmas. Acquired by the Prince of Wales (later Edward VII) in 1862. He had it rebuilt by 1870. George V bequeathed it to his eldest son, Edward VIII, who contemplated

5 WINDSOR CASTLE

4 KENSINGTON PALACE

7 FROGMORE

1 BUCKINGHAM PALACE

selling it. Instead, on his Abdication in 1936, he sold his life interest in Sandringham and Balmoral to his brother in exchange for £25,000 a year. The 20,000-acre estate produces enough revenue to run the house as well as Balmoral. The Queen's racing stud is here.

10. Wood Farm
A secluded house on the Sandringham estate where the epileptic Prince John, the youngest son of King George V and Queen Mary, lived with his nanny until his death at the age of 13, in 1919. It is often used by the Queen on visits to Norfolk to avoid opening the big house.

11. Anmer Hall
A Georgian ten-bedroom house on the Sandringham estate, three miles east of the main house. It was updated in 2013 by the Duke and Duchess of Cambridge, who use it as their family home. Prince George attends a Montessori nursery near by.

·······················

SCOTLAND
12. Balmoral Castle
(*privately owned by the Queen*)
Partly open to the public when the Queen is not in residence
Balmoral Castle in Aberdeenshire is where the Queen and Prince Philip spend every summer holiday from the end of July until early October. Queen Victoria rented it from the 3rd Earl of Aberdeen in 1848, and bought it in 1852. By 1856 the castle had been completely rebuilt. It now covers an area of about 49,000 acres, is a working estate, including grouse moors, forestry and farmland, as well as managed herds of deer, Highland cattle and ponies.

13. Birkhall
A house on the Balmoral estate near Loch Muick built in 1715 that Prince Charles uses as his Scottish base. He spent his second honeymoon here with the Duchess of Cornwall in 2005. From 1930 it was lent to the Duke and Duchess of York, so the Queen spent childhood summers here. She also spent part of her honeymoon here, as well as summers with her young family before becoming Queen.

14. Craigowan Lodge
A seven-bedroom house on the Balmoral estate which the royal family use when they do not want to open up the castle. When the Queen is staying at the castle, it is used by her private secretary.

15. Palace of Holyroodhouse, Edinburgh
(*owned by the nation*) *Open to the public*
The Queen's official Scottish residence, she spends a week here every July. The original palace was built in 1501. Mary Queen of Scots spent much time here.

16. Castle of Mey
(*owned by the Castle of Mey Trust*) *Open to the public in summer*
On the mainland opposite Orkney. The Queen Mother found it almost derelict in the first months of her widowhood, bought it privately and restored it. Prince Charles stays for a few days each year.

GLOUCESTERSHIRE
17. Highgrove
(*owned by the Duchy of Cornwall*) *Gardens opened by arrangement*
Prince Charles's country home in Gloucestershire. It was bought by the Duchy of Cornwall in 1980 from Maurice Macmillan (son of Harold). The prince has embellished the exterior with classical pilasters that he designed. He has created magnificent gardens here.

18. Gatcombe Park
(*privately bought by the Queen for her daughter*)
Near Minchinhampton and six miles from Highgrove, it has been Princess Anne's main home since 1976. It has an estate of 730 acres where she holds the annual Festival of British Eventing in August as well as other horse trials.

NEWS UK ARCHIVE; BBC; LICHFIELD/GETTY IMAGES

▶ **Talking to the animals**
The Queen chats to one of her pets on her return from Balmoral in 1986

THE ROYAL CORGIS — A QUEEN'S BEST FRIENDS

▶ **The dog with the golden lead**
Monty the corgi accompanies the Queen as she takes part in the James Bond video made for the 2012 London Olympics

▶ **Steadfast companions**
The Queen with two of her corgis on the Balmoral estate in 1971

Whether on duty or off, the Queen keeps her dogs near, writes Valentine Low

The Queen's corgis are an instantly recognisable part of her public image. From newspaper cartoons to the video she made with Daniel Craig for the 2012 London Olympics — in which the now-deceased corgi Monty made a cameo appearance — when a corgi appears, the Queen is never far behind. They even play a crucial role in kickstarting the plot in Alan Bennett's literary fantasy about the Queen, *The Uncommon Reader*.

Yet for all the Queen's devotion to her corgis — and her dorgis, a cross between a dachshund and a corgi — it would be wrong to think that she is a one-breed woman.

There are labradors too, and spaniels: the Queen takes an active interest in the Sandringham kennels, and in her prime was regarded as a highly proficient handler of gundogs.

Her first dog, however, the one that inspired her love of animals, was none of these; it was a cairn terrier, given to her by her uncle, the Prince of Wales, the future Edward VIII. Princess Elizabeth was three years old at the time.

The first corgi to enter her life was called Dookie, bought by her father, George VI, in 1933. Others followed, generation after generation of them; one of the most notable was Susan, the matriarch of the dynasty. On the Queen's wedding day, when she and Prince Philip were driven in an open carriage from Buckingham Palace to Waterloo station for the start of their honeymoon, Susan travelled with them, snuggled up under a rug. At Waterloo she stole the show by tumbling out first on to the red carpet that awaited them.

Being a royal pet is, naturally, not a life short of privilege. At Buckingham Palace the dogs sleep in their own room, in wicker baskets raised a few inches off the floor to avoid draughts. Whenever she can, the Queen exercises them herself, and it is said that if she is wearing a headscarf when she comes into

ANWAR HUSSEIN/ LISA SHERIDAN/GETTY IMAGES; TIMES NEWSPAPERS

a room they sense that a walk is imminent and will scamper about excitedly.

The former royal chef Darren McGrady, who worked for the Queen for 11 years, once described how the corgis would be served only the finest fare. "One day it would be chuck steak, which we boiled and served with finely chopped, boiled cabbage and white rice. The next they'd have poached chicken or liver. Or rabbits shot by William or Harry that we'd clean, cook, debone and chop for the dogs."

If the dogs could be unruly, it seemed to be just the way the Queen liked it. "They chase rabbits like mad," the Queen's cousin Margaret Rhodes said once. "There are a lot of rabbits around Balmoral, certainly, and the Queen gets excited with the dogs chasing rabbits, egging them on. Telling them to keep going — 'Keep on going!'"

There could be trouble, though. Susan once bit the royal clock winder, and also attacked one of the palace sentries. Another bit a policeman.

Last year it emerged that the Queen's present dogs — two corgis, Holly and Willow, and two dorgis, Candy and Vulcan — could be her last. Monty Roberts, an informal adviser to the Queen, said she had declined his offer to find a puppy after the death of Monty. He told *Vanity Fair* magazine: "She didn't want any more young dogs. She didn't want to leave any young dog behind. She wanted to put an end to it."

"
The Queen gets excited with the dogs chasing rabbits, egging them on: 'Keep on going!'

◄ **Taking the lead**
The Queen arrives at Aberdeen airport with a trio of dogs, ready to start her holiday in Balmoral in 1974

▲ **Pure devotion**
The Queen at the Royal Windsor Horse Show, 1973

◄ **Playing house**
Princess Elizabeth and Princess Margaret in the Little House — their two-thirds size cottage in the grounds of the Royal Lodge, Windsor — in 1936

◄ **A royal walkies**
The Queen and her mother walk their dogs at Sandringham in November 1956

ALL IN A DAY'S WORK

From letter-reading to private audiences, investitures, visits and receptions, the Queen's commitment

1

2

6

7

8

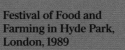

1 Round the houses
Exploring Legoland
Windsor with Prince
Philip in 2003

2 Record breaker
Attending to her
daily red boxes on
September 9, 2015 —
the day she became
Britain's longest-
reigning monarch

3 Snout and about
Inspecting a pig at the

Festival of Food and
Farming in Hyde Park,
London, 1989

4 Caravan, Ma'am
Visiting a caravan
factory in Bristol
during her Diamond
Jubilee tour in 2012

5 Burning interest
Watching a chemistry
demonstration while
opening Parmiter's
School, Watford, in 1981

6 Winning them over
Captain Alastair Cook
introduces his team to
the Queen before an
Ashes match between
England and Australia
at Lord's in July 2013

7 New dimension
The Queen and the
Duke of Edinburgh
sporting 3D glasses
during a visit to
the University of
Sheffield in 2010

8 Market day
Meeting a fishmonger
in Cork in 2011 during
her historic Irish tour

9 Golden girl
Awarding the CBE to
Olympic champion
Jessica Ennis in 2013

10 Cup holder
Touring Seoul during
the first state visit to
South Korea by
a British monarch

▶ **Good going**
With her racing
manager John
Warren on Derby
day at Epsom in
2012, the first day
of her four-day
Diamond Jubilee
celebrations

Since her grandfather George V regaled her with tales of royal glory on the turf, the Queen has had a zest for horse racing. She is rarely more at ease than at the stable or the track, says Julian Muscat

HER PASSION AND HER SANCTUARY

◀ **Firm favourite**
At Sandringham
in 1964, with her
horse Betsy

On the morning of her Coronation, Princess Elizabeth was asked by a lady-in-waiting how she was feeling. She replied that she was very well: her trainer had just called to relate that her horse Aureole had completed his Derby preparation with a pleasing gallop.

Four days later, on her first visit to Epsom, she watched in a state of high excitement as Aureole finished runner-up to Pinza. Aureole's noble effort is still the closest she has come to winning the Derby. Her inaugural win in a Classic would come four years later, her homebred filly Carrozza taking the Oaks at Epsom, ridden by Lester Piggott.

The Queen's relationship with racing is not so much a casual acquaintance as a full-

blooded embrace. Racecourses are her sanctuary, where she can be herself. She is often at Newbury's spring meeting in April, when she is in her element. Unlike the Derby or Ascot, where she is invariably a focal point, here the Queen will simply dissolve into the mix. She moves around without overt security. She can be like any other owner as she assesses runners in the paddock before making her way through crowds towards the grandstand. During her visits to the races the Queen radiates happiness, in contrast to her oft-sombre appearance in the line of duty.

She would doubtless have spent more time on the racecourse if circumstances had permitted. She once mused that but for the Archbishop of Canterbury she would have

been off in her plane every Sunday to Long-champ, in Paris, where her filly Highclere galloped to victory in the 1974 Prix de Diane.

If her zest for racing is plain, she reveals more about herself when visiting her horses at her trainers' stables. She wants no fuss; she wants only to see her thoroughbreds going through their paces. Her insistence on infor-mality encourages her trainers to treat her in kind. Most of them do just that — especially Richard Hannon, who served her for 16 years until his retirement in 2013, and whose jovial insouciance the Queen found particularly amusing. On one occasion, when Hannon tried to communicate with a rider recently arrived from India who understood no Eng-lish, he turned to the Queen in exasperation and asked whether she could speak Indian. When she replied that she couldn't, Hannon rejoined: "Well you ought to, Ma'am. You ruled the place for long enough."

Her love of racing surfaces spontaneously, as it did in 2008, when her horse Free Agent ended a nine-year royal drought at Ascot. There the Queen stood, punching the air before hot-footing it down to the winner's enclosure. "It was as if she was 20 years old," recalled her bloodstock and racing adviser John Warren, who succeeded his father-in-law, the 7th Earl of Carnarvon, to the post on the latter's death in 2001. "The rest of us were struggling to keep up."

Warren is well placed to amplify the Queen's passion. "It didn't take me long to realise that her fundamental interest revolves utterly and totally around the horse itself," he said. "The depth of her knowledge is extraordinary. Nobody else in the country has been breeding racehorses for more than 60 years."

Princess Elizabeth was three years old when George V regaled his granddaughter with the story of Scuttle carrying the royal silks to victory in the 1928 One Thousand Guineas at Newmarket. A year later she was given Peggy, her first pony. However, her love of racing escalated in 1942, when her father owned a pair of superior racehorses whose exploits would bring him the accolade of Britain's leading owner. In the spring of that year George VI took his daughter to Fred Darling's stables in Beckhampton, Wiltshire, to cast her eye over Big Game and Sun Chariot. The two horses would win four of the five Classics and Princess Elizabeth, then 16, was so smitten on touching their silken coats that she would not wash her hands for hours afterwards.

To the public, the Queen will always be synonymous with Royal Ascot. She hosts a lunch at Windsor Castle on each of the meeting's five days and is always anxious to arrive at the racecourse punctually. She has savoured 22 Royal Ascot winners in the distinctive purple and red royal silks, among them Expansive in the 1979 Ribblesdale Stakes, a race Her Majesty has won three

> The Queen's relationship with racing is not so much a casual acquaintance but a full-blooded embrace

times. They came thick and fast in the early years, when the Royal Studs were not in competition with the plethora of Middle Eastern potentates who have patronised British racing since the early 1980s. There are limits to what she can spend on bloodstock: the royal horses are all paid for from the Queen's private purse.

Nevertheless, despite front-line successes becoming increasingly elusive, the Queen's interest has intensified with the passing years. In her early eighties she decided to overhaul bloodlines within the Royal Studs. The move is paying dividends: three of her five best racehorses last season were from this new blood.

For the Queen, however, it is not all about the big occasion. It is about giving every one of her horses the best possible opportunity to express its potential. Her biggest triumph to date came in 2013 when Estimate galloped away with Royal Ascot's signature race, the Gold Cup. It marked the first victory for a British monarch in the race's 207-year history, after which the Queen revealed that it was the race she had yearned to win above all others.

◀ **Royal silks**
With Ryan Moore, who rode the Queen's horse Estimate to victory in the Gold Cup at Ascot in 2013

▲ **Winning smile**
Congratulating her horse Expansive, which won the Ribblesdale Stakes at Ascot in 1979, with Lord Carnarvon (right)

▶ **First filly**
The Queen leads in her filly Carrozza after it won the Oaks at Epsom in 1957, ridden by Lester Piggott

THE ROYAL GARDEN PARTY

Daniel Finkelstein recalls his day on the Buckingham Palace lawn

'We do these things very well," my grandmother used to say when I was a boy and we watched a royal event on television. I thought it was a fitting comment; it seemed to me true, as far as I could make out from the telly, and I took pride in it.

Yet looking back, I think the most interesting word in the sentence was "we". My grandmother was born in Poland, as was my father. My mum was born in Berlin and brought up in Amsterdam. So it is interesting that the word "we" came naturally.

I think of King John as being part of my history, even though around the time of Magna Carta, my family was celebrating the crowning of Daniel of Galicia as King of Halych-Volhynia — give or take a hundred years or so. I think this is part of the Queen's achievement, and her importance. She has somehow made a diverse people — with an incredibly varied history — think of themselves as "we".

The royal garden party is one of the things my grandmother was talking about when she praised how we do things. I didn't experience it on television, however. I went.

It is almost 20 years ago now, while I was working for Conservative Central Office. I knew I hadn't been selected to go because of any special distinction. The office got some invitations and it was my turn. Still, it was nice to get the stiff, embossed card from the Lord Chamberlain. And I would definitely have put it on the mantelpiece if we'd had one. As it was, I left it nonchalantly on the radiator shelf, face up, just in case anyone came to mend the radiator and might be so impressed that they mended it more carefully.

When my wife and I arrived at Buckingham Palace, there was a queue to get in. Quite a long one. This was my first clue to something I should have realised earlier. Indeed,

I probably knew it, if I had been bothered to think it through. Each party has many thousands of guests. About 8,000 each. Of course they do, or I would not have been invited.

However obvious and necessary this may be, it does, at first, seem a little disappointing. Yet as it turns out, it isn't a disappointing event. How could it be? Even walking across the gravel at the palace was exciting.

In order for a garden party to be anything other than a scrum, it has to be carefully organised. And fortunately, it is. Guests are encouraged to stand in lanes and a number are selected to meet members of the royal family. We were not, but because the Queen was meeting someone very close to where we were standing, we felt included in the conversation. It was quite cleverly done.

The whole royal family were present — the Queen Mother, for instance, was there — so you felt part of a special occasion, despite the number of guests. And after the lanes and collecting tea you could stroll round the gardens, which meant you weren't standing in a crowd the whole time.

Watching the Queen work is fascinating. Each encounter is a highlight in the life of the person she is meeting, while, for her, being just a few moments in the schedule. These are moments the visitor will never forget and she won't remember even by suppertime. She has to do the same things, say the same things, over and over again.

Yet it never seems like that. She is supremely professional, warm without being less than regal, interested without exhausting herself with small talk. I feel very fortunate to have been invited. The sense of being "we" is strong within me.

▶ **Green cards**
A garden party at the palace in 1957. About 8,000 guests attend each event

THE LEGACY
A NEW ELIZABETHAN AGE

The Queen on September 9, 2015, the day she became Britain's longest reigning monarch, waves from a carriage window at Edinburgh's Waverly Station, after boarding a steam train to inaugurate the £294 million Scottish Borders Railway

▶ **Glory days**
Prince Philip, the
Queen, the Duchess
of Cornwall and
the Duchess of
Cambridge on
board the *Spirit of
Chartwell* on
a very wet day at
the Diamond
Jubilee pageant on
the Thames

REINVENTING THE MONARCHY

JOHN STILLWELL/GETTY IMAGES

After a decade of crisis, the Queen herself oversaw the royal family's renaissance — and has seen her approval ratings reach new heights, writes Damian Whitworth

The moment during her reign when the Queen's ability to reinvent the monarchy for the modern age was demonstrated most cleverly came when she starred as a Bond girl. Her agreement to participate in the opening ceremony at the 2012 Olympic Games with Daniel Craig was a master stroke. As she and 007 appeared to parachute into the stadium, the audience let out a gasp audible to the ceremony's television audience of 900 million. The six-minute film, showing the Queen and Craig in the grandeur of Buckingham Palace, then their stunt doubles throwing themselves out of a helicopter above the stadium, was a fusion of ancient royal mystique with modern wit.

The Queen's reign has spanned the TV age but she would not have considered anything so bold even a few years earlier. That she could provide the biggest surprise on a night of theatrical wonders was testimony to how shrewdly she had led the steady rebranding of "The Firm" after years when the share price had been heavily depressed.

In 2012, her Diamond Jubilee year, the Queen's approval ratings reached new heights. Ninety per cent of Britons said they were satisfied with how she did her job. Only 7 per cent said they were dissatisfied — the sort of figures of which elected heads of state can only dream. This marked a significant upturn in her popularity from the tumultuous 1990s when the monarchy reeled from one crisis to another, the public began to take a dim view and there was a rise in republican sentiment.

From those dark days the Queen has spearheaded a remarkable comeback in the fortunes of her family, showing the monarchy's ability to evolve, and securing its place in the future of these islands. As *The Times* put it during the Diamond Jubilee: "It is easy to forget, in the summer of 2012, that half a generation ago the royal house of Windsor had stretched the people's patience close to breaking point." An event by a republican

The crowd-puller
A packed Mall during the Queen's Diamond Jubilee on June 5, 2012

THE QUEEN AT NINETY

▲ **Refreshing the brand**
The Duchess of Cambridge and the Queen watch a children's sports event in Nottingham during the Diamond Jubilee year

pressure group attracted only 60 people and chants of "Lizzie, Lizzie, Lizzie, Out, Out, Out" were drowned out by "God Save the Queen".

Sir David Attenborough, who was born a couple of weeks after the Queen, has joked that people often acquire "national treasure" status because they have been around such a long time. It is true that the Queen's longevity has contributed to her appeal. She has been on the throne throughout the lives of the majority of her subjects and as the years have elapsed between past tawdry events and the most recent images of her indefatigable dutifulness, there is a growing appreciation of her

as a comforting presence. Through financial meltdown and political crisis, she has remained constant, calm and rarely emotional — unless one of her horses is winning. She has ploughed on with public appearances, private audiences and official briefings.

It is easier for a nation to feel well disposed towards a happy family, and as time has passed this one has looked so much happier. Camilla Parker Bowles, once so unpopular that she was pelted with rolls in a supermarket, has not only been brought into the fold but has been able to marry the heir to the throne and win public acceptance. More than

that: with her down-to-earth humour and light touch, the Duchess of Cornwall proves popular when she accompanies the prince and helps him appear contented and relaxed.

The Duke of Cambridge has gone a step farther and married into the middle class. Kate Middleton's parents, former British Airways employees, run a mail-order party business and she has ancestors who were Geordie coalminers. Thus the younger royals have refreshed the brand and offer optimism about the future leadership of the Commonwealth.

The 2011 wedding of Prince William to his Catherine saw a million people on the streets

of London and hundreds of millions watching worldwide. It was a feelgood event at a time when the country had been mired in the longest period of austerity in living memory. George and Charlotte have completed the picture of a fully functional family that has rediscovered its mojo and is closer to the rest of the population than before. George, born to live in a palace, spends many weekends with his mother's parents who have proved hands-on grandparents in a way that a future king has probably never experienced before.

The maturing of Prince Harry, who shows humour and much of his mother's humanity on tours and in charity work, has helped him to become a popular member of the clan.

The royal family plots its longterm strategy carefully and has benefited from a professionalisation of its household. Though the family is traditionally comfortable surrounded by aristocrats the Queen's key advisers in recent years have been her private secretary, Sir Christopher Geidt, and his predecessor Lord Janvrin, former diplomats. The household has embraced social media but has not lost its ability to pull off the best pageantry in the world. First there was the wedding, then, in 2012, the Diamond Jubilee weekend. This extravaganza

▲ **New drive**
Prince William chauffeurs his bride from the palace after their wedding reception on April 29, 2011

▲ **The little prince**
Prince George on his first day at nursery school in Norfolk, January 6, 2016

▲ **Regal heights**
The RAF's Red Arrows execute a flypast for the Diamond Jubilee

▲ **Gung ho**
Prince Charles and the Duchess of Cornwall take part, with gusto, in a parachute game at a youth festival in Guernsey, July 2012

▼ **Standing
on ceremony**
The Queen
formally opens the
London Olympics
on July 27, 2012

▶ **Bond girl**
Her stunt double
parachutes into the
Olympic Stadium

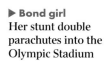

" She was fun,
incredibly game.
She improvised a
little bit. She was
supposed to be
sitting at the desk
and she asked if she
could write, so she
pretended to write

DANIEL CRAIG ON THE
OLYMPICS BOND SKIT

concluded with a service at St Paul's and a
balcony appearance at the palace that featured
only six family members: the Queen, the
Prince of Wales, the Duchess of Cornwall, the
Duke and Duchess of Cambridge and Prince
Harry. The tableau sent a message that here
was a streamlined unit focused on keeping the
family business going.

Earlier a 1,000-strong flotilla processed
down the Thames on a miserably wet day
when onlookers and monarch were united in
a soggy, dogged desire to celebrate the glorious
nuttiness of being British. At the celebratory
concert Madness sang "Our house in the
middle of one's street" from the roof of Buckingham Palace. Britain felt like one nation.

When the Queen became the UK's longest-reigning monarch she was less keen to
celebrate. A moment arrived on the afternoon
of Wednesday, September 9, last year when
she had been on the throne for 23,226 days,
16 hours and 23 minutes, passing Queen
Victoria's record. For various reasons, not
least that her accession was bound up with
the death of her father, she was reluctant to
make any fuss, but eventually agreed to open
the Scottish Borders Railway that day.

Standing next to Scotland's first minister,
Nicola Sturgeon, after journeying by steam
train from Edinburgh to Tweedbank, the
Queen alluded briefly to her new place in the
history books. "Many, including you, first
minister, have also kindly noted another sig-
nificance attaching to today, although it is not
one to which I have ever aspired. Inevitably,
a long life can pass by many milestones; my
own is no exception. But I thank you all, and
the many others at home and overseas, for
your touching messages of great kindness."

PLAYING PIANISSIMO

The Queen famously holds no artistic opinions — but she knows her music, says **Richard Morrison**

The modern British monarchy is not greatly renowned for its patronage of the arts. George V's response when someone asked him why *La bohème* was his favourite opera — "It's the shortest" — is seen as typical of a dynasty whose sense of duty compels its scions to sit through a vast amount of "culture" without necessarily showing too much enthusiasm for it.

Over the past decade, however, I've had the privilege of glimpsing (albeit in a very occasional way) what goes on behind the scenes at Buckingham Palace, and a very different picture emerges. My own connection started not long after the Queen appointed Peter Maxwell Davies as her Master of Music. That in itself was a startling decision. The ancient office of Master of the Queen's (or King's) Music had come to seem more of a ceremonial sinecure for an establishment worthy than a platform for someone who was going to champion music vigorously in the highest circles.

That all changed with the Queen's elevation of "Max" in 2004. Fiercely republican (in his youth, anyway), left-wing and gay, he also wrote music that was often abrasive and frequently disturbing. He was also mischievously outspoken. Suddenly a man at the heart of the royal household was demanding to know why Her Majesty's government was not doing more to support Britain's orchestras and choirs, and why the Queen's ministers seemed to be acting in ways that diminished or even eliminated music and the arts in schools.

He was not, of course, claiming to articulate what the Queen thought. Yet the fact that he spoke out had a galvanising effect. And during his time as Master there were notable innovations.

One was the Queen's Medal for Music. Music was, and is, a huge profession in the UK. Hundreds of thousands of people earn their living by composing, performing, teaching, publishing, broadcasting and writing about music. Yet there was no official annual award to acknowledge someone who had set an outstanding example.

The Queen rectified this in Max's first year as Master. He pulled together a small committee of people who could make recommendations (I was honoured to be part of it) and each year since 2005 the Queen's Medal for Music has been awarded to an outstanding individual.

Some other cultural innovations instigated by royal command proved even more surprising. Perhaps the most eye-popping were the Prom at the Palace and its pop counterpart, the Party at the Palace. It's impossible to imagine a monarch before Elizabeth II throwing open her back garden to two massive concerts in quick proximity. Yet that's what happened in June 2002 to mark her Golden Jubilee. In all, 24,000 people won tickets in a lottery to enter the gardens and hear a line-up of performers that included Kiri Te Kanawa and Mstislav Rostropovich on the classical side and Paul McCartney and Elton John among the pop luminaries. A further million people were estimated to be watching each concert live on big screens in The Mall and 200 million viewing on television.

The Queen famously does not have artistic opinions — or at least none that she expresses in public. Except that she clearly does. She has spent the best part of 90 years listening to music, opening exhibitions and watching actors, dancers and singers around the world. And she has lived through many different artistic epochs. When she was a child Elgar wrote music for her. Later, she became friendly with such creative giants as Benjamin Britten and Lucian Freud. She was born five days before the premiere of Puccini's *Turandot*, and 18 months before the first "talkie" hit the cinemas. Her teenage years were the heyday of the big bands. Yet she has lived to see rock, punk and rap, *Star Wars* and YouTube.

You don't experience all that without forming views on artistic taste and quality. Anyone who has eavesdropped on the Queen in conversation with artists or performers will know that she asks shrewd questions and relishes illuminating replies. She certainly knows what she enjoys — and what she doesn't. Maxwell Davies discovered that when he entered into a discussion with her about modern, atonal harmony. "The Queen doesn't like dissonant music," he told *The Times* in 2014. "She has stated that very plainly. I have discussed these technical aspects with her and she knows what I am talking about. She's as bright as a button. And I think it was a very good thing that she makes her position clear. You know where you stand. We all do."

◀ **Andy Warhol, 1985**
The Royal Collection

"I want to be as famous as the Queen of England," Andy Warhol once said. The cult hipster worshipped at the shrine of celebrity. Hardly surprising then, that he should have turned eventually to our monarch as his subject: so instantly recognisable, so impenetrably remote. He created this silkscreen in 1985, basing it on a photograph that had been officially released for the 1977 Silver Jubilee year. A special royal edition was produced, sprinkled with diamond dust that twinkled and winked in the light. What may be more surprising is that the monarch herself appears to be a fan of the famously queeny Warhol. A set of prints from this series was purchased and added to the Royal Collection three years ago.

A SOVEREIGN IMAGE

Rachel Campbell-Johnston highlights some of the key likenesses of the most represented figure in the world, from the much loved to the highly controversial

'I have to be seen to be believed." It may sound like a quote from some Lewis Carroll character, but actually it was Queen Elizabeth II who uttered these words. So perhaps it should not be remotely surprising to discover that she is the single most represented individual in the world.

It's not just the stamps, coins and bank notes that have made her image ubiquitous. A long line of royal portrait commissions extends back across her 90 years. It was 1933 when a little blonde four-year-old Princess Lilibet first posed in white frills for the then fashionable Philip de László. Some 150 more official portraits have followed — not to mention the thousands of unofficial images that have also been created, using anything from traditional pigments through car parts to piles of jelly beans.

The reign of a woman who was born in the crux year of the General Strike has spanned a period of all but unprecedented social change. Her portraits reflect this. The newly crowned monarch whom Pietro Annigoni presents in all her serenely unassailable glamour is the same one who scowls like a fierce granny, five decades later, from a patch of canvas painted by Lucian Freud. The transition bears testimony not just to time's passing but to changing public perceptions.

BRIAN COOKE/REDFERNS/GETTY; ANNIGONI//CAMERA PRESS; NATIONAL PORTRAIT GALLERY; TIM GRAHAM/GETTY IMAGES

▲ **Sex Pistols artwork, 1977**
In conjunction with Jamie Reid
Punk was at its height. Public perceptions of royalty were being reassessed. A growing familiarity led to a never-before-dared irreverence, nowhere more notoriously than in this picture that featured on promotional posters for the Sex Pistols single *God Save The Queen*. The designer and self-proclaimed anarchist adds torn newsprint to an iconic Peter Grugeon photo, mimicking the style of a ransom note. It has remained a firm favourite with anti-authoritarian protesters.

▲ **Pietro Annigoni, 1956**
The Fishmongers' Hall, London
Probably the public's favourite portrait of the Queen. Annigoni gave her a romantic makeover as he painted her in her Garter robes. "When I was a child, I used to spend hours looking out of the windows," the Queen told Annigoni. "I loved watching the people and the cars in The Mall." The artist recalled her face lit up with the almost childlike expression he captured in a portrait that speaks of a person who is at once a beautiful young woman and a grand regal figure.

Royal portraits hold up a mirror to all those who gaze at them. The regal aura that surrounds Cecil Beaton's coronation picture speaks of a deference that harks back to medieval days, when belief in the divine right of kings was entrenched.

An increasingly relaxed image of the Queen was propagated in the Sixties by the press. Then the Seventies saw the production of Jamie Reid's iconoclastic poster design for a single by the Sex Pistols. Growing familiarity had signalled the beginning of a new irreverence.

But if the royal portrait reflects public perceptions, what can it show us of the real character of the Queen? It's virtually impossible for a painter in just a few controlled sittings to probe beneath the façade of so professional a monarch. The attempts have been many and various, and often pretty dreadful. In our modern photographic era, it is probably the camera that has succeeded best. But the Queen keeps her own counsel. She never comments on the pictures produced, although some portraits hang in the royal collection and one of Warhol's prints was used as her official portrait in the Washington embassy. She remains an enigma. And all we are left with is the images. We have to decide for ourselves if we believe what we see.

▲ **Michael Leonard, 1985-86**
National Portrait Gallery
Commissioned by *Reader's Digest* on the Queen's 60th birthday, this portrait is less a picture of remote regal celebrity than a head of state in the guise of housewife. Leonard's aim was to create a picture that would "play down the remoteness of Her Majesty's special position". But for all its apparent homeliness (and Spark the dog beside her), this hyperrealist confection is as artificial as any formal portrait, as carefully composed as every curl on her immaculately coiffed head.

▲ **Andrew Festing, 1999**
Royal Hospital Chelsea
In portraying the Queen in the robes she wears for the State Opening of Parliament, Festing presents her as a pillar of the society for which she serves as the symbolic head. In the background stand two of the residents of the Royal Hospital, where this portrait now hangs. Beyond hangs a monumental Van Dyck portrait of Charles I. Our monarch is portrayed as the proud inheritor of an ancient British office, even as she is shown as the benign matriarch of our nation.

◀ **Lucian Freud, 2000-01**
Royal Collection

No portrait of the Queen has divided opinion quite like this small, uncompromising oil. Freud has scrutinised our monarch, seeking out the facts that are too easily left hidden under a veneer of deference. He offers not an idealised symbol but the face of a stoical old woman worn down by long years of duty. Her iconic crown — the Diamond Diadem, worn for the State Opening of Parliament and depicted on banknotes and postage stamps — has been plonked on her grey curls with all the aplomb of a piece of dressing-up-box plastic. It was added as an afterthought during the sitting. Unflattering travesty or profound testimony to the psychological truth? This portrait presents a wilfully provocative conundrum.

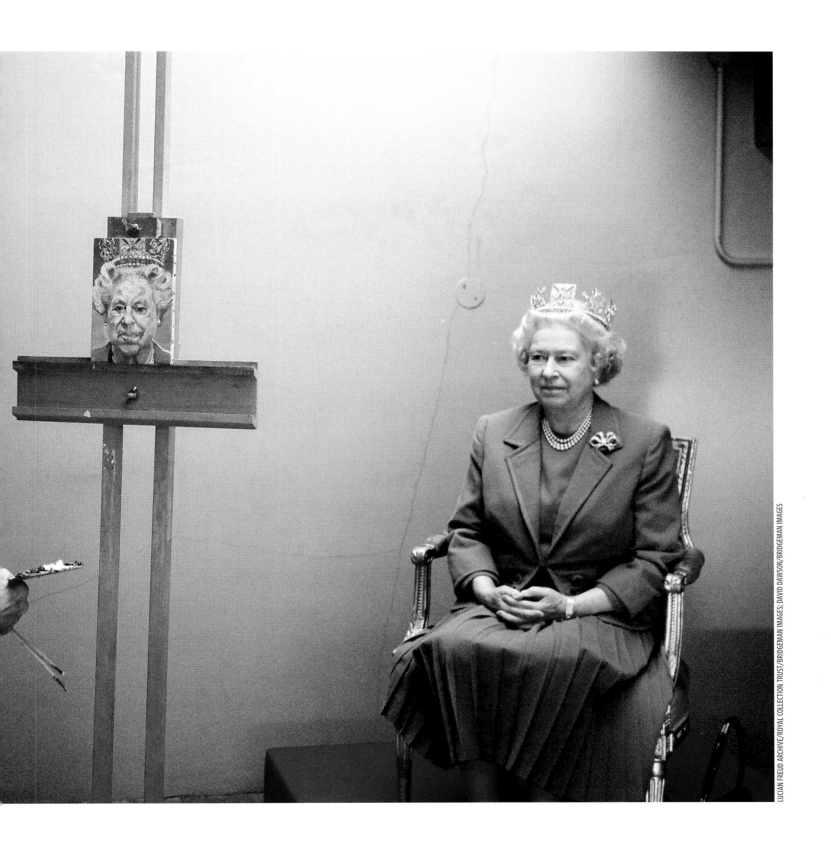

▲ **John Wonnacott, 2000**
National Portrait Gallery
This massive (12ft high) group portrait sets the Queen in a relaxed family context — the monarch as mother. Despite the splendour of the White Drawing Room, it's relatively informal; the pile of corgis emphasises it. But it also carries a dynastic message. The Queen Mother is the matriarchal lynchpin. Our monarch and her consort seem almost withdrawn. Prince Charles waits on the sidelines, while his heir takes a foreground slot, his sleeves rolled up for the job.

AN HOUR IN HER PRESENCE

The story behind the only official portrait of the Queen in 2012, by **Rachel Campbell-Johnston**

How does a portraitist set about capturing a true sense of the Queen's character? The Australian-born Ralph Heimans was the only artist chosen to paint an official portrait of the Queen in her Diamond Jubilee year. The Australian National Portrait Gallery wanted an image for a display, and he had already done an acclaimed portrait of Princess Mary of Denmark.

"Royal portraiture is often formulaic," says Heimans. "It is often quite static and two-dimensional. It doesn't deal with concepts. Images of power can undermine the truth of the picture, of the sense of the actual person beneath the trappings of office. But it's the story of what they might be feeling that fascinates me.

"I wanted to describe an imagined moment," he says. "The Queen would be alone, at night, in Westminster Abbey, standing at the precise spot where she had been crowned.

"I thought a narrative would offer the public a chance to engage: to try to imagine what the Queen might be thinking or feeling. I wanted her expression to be quite nuanced and reflective. I hoped the heaviness of the robe would evoke her burden of office. And I wanted her to be alone. No one but a Queen can understand what it feels like to be a Queen. I wanted to capture a sense of her singular existence."

His proposal was submitted to the palace. Ten months later he was told the Queen would sit for him for an hour. At meetings it was discussed what she would wear. "I suggested her coronation robe," he says, "but it was decided that her parliamentary robe would be better. As a portraitist, you have to come in with a vision, but then you have to adapt and be receptive. And her decision felt fortuitous. The parliamentary robe is almost more symbolic."

On March 25, 2012, Heimans arrived at the palace. "An hour is very brief. I came in with a clear image of what I wanted to achieve. But what I had not accounted for was the sense of her presence. It was extraordinary to watch her approach, her long robe carried by footmen, an entourage flanking her. She was sparkling with diamonds. Then as she got nearer I was confronted by her as a physical person, a woman with soulful eyes. I got a huge sense of her humanity. It was something I hadn't anticipated.

"I bowed. I had never bowed to anyone before. She had just returned from Australia, so we spoke about that, then I asked her to imagine she was alone in the abbey. After that the sitting was conducted mainly in silence. It was better, because what I was seeking was something reflective. I took photographs. She's so used to sitting, she knew what I needed: I couldn't ask her to look down, but that's the pose you naturally adopt when thinking about the past. But the robe was heavy, and after ten minutes she would have to sit and rest. I was told that if I could finish early it would be much appreciated so I ended ten minutes before the official time was up. She was happy. 'Now I've got time to walk the corgis,' she said."

Heimans did dozens of studies before embarking on the vast 250 x 342cm canvas. "It was the largest painting I had ever undertaken. I had to erect scaffolding. It was also the most challenging from the point of view of the composition, the perspective and perhaps most of all the emotion."

The Queen famously never comments on finished works. But Heimans received another commission from the Royal Collection shortly afterwards so he assumes she was happy. His portrait was a huge success in Australia — the gallery had an unprecedented number of visitors. "People seemed to respond to its emotional message. Because it was so large they felt as if they were entering into its space."

Later, Heimans' portrait was hung in Westminster Abbey where, in 2013, it was defaced by a protester. The artist, appalled, feared the face might have been targeted. "The face is the soul of the painting and is very hard to recreate," he said.

The damage, however, was not lasting and the portrait has since been cleaned and rehung.

RALPH HEIMANS

▲ **Likeness-minded** Ralph Heimans with his painting *The Coronation Theatre, Westminster Abbey: Portrait of Her Majesty Queen Elizabeth II, 2012*

Elizabeth II A remarkably hard act to follow

The Queen may come to be seen as the most successful monarch in British history. Her heirs will have a lot to live up to, says Ben Macintyre

One way to assess the legacy of Britain's longest-reigning monarch is to look back to where her story started. *The Times* of April 21, 1926, carried a very small announcement on page 14, between a report on ructions in the German cabinet and another on the progress of the economy bill: "The Duchess of York was safely delivered of a Princess at 2.40 this morning. Both mother and daughter are doing well." The baby would go on to become Elizabeth II.

Hers has been an extraordinary reign, not just for its longevity but for its strange and effective combination of consistency and adaptability, tradition and subtle innovation. She will leave the monarchy more secure than many would have predicted, but her very success leaves her heirs a problem: she will be a remarkably hard act to follow.

The newspaper on the day of her birth announcement reflected a secure, stratified society, a Britain that was still imperial and colonial; it was complacently and deeply royalist, confident in its collective identity. Reporting on the royal family was demure, discreet and, above all, deferential.

The Britain Elizabeth came to rule in 1952 was still recognisable as the one she had been born into. The news of her accession reached her in Kenya, then still firmly under British rule despite rumblings of rebellion. She had every reason to expect that she would rule in much the same way as her father and grandfather. It did not turn out that way.

As she observed in her Golden Jubilee speech of 2002: "Since 1952 I have witnessed the transformation of the international landscape ... matched by no less rapid developments at home, in the devolved shape of our nation, in the structure of society, in technology and communications, in our work and in the way we live."

The London of 1952 still had trams and smog. Churchill was still prime minister, and British troops were still fighting in Korea. The mathematician Alan Turing was forced to undergo hormone treatment to avoid prison for his homosexuality. Britain remained an intensely traditional, old-fashioned realm with a monarchy that was little changed, in most important respects, since the time of Victoria.

Over the ensuing years, royalty was tested by war, tragedy and scandal; it was transformed by public curiosity, social mobility and imperial decline; above all, the habit of reverential discretion has now almost disappeared, replaced by attitudes more questioning but also, perhaps, more intelligent.

Elizabeth II will bequeath a monarchy that has become a professional operation. She has been the first monarch in history not to impose her personal likes and dislikes on the institution; indeed, her real personality has remained, for most of her subjects, an enigma. She may have ruled for longer than any other British monarch, but few of her subjects can remember anything she has said. In the intrusive, fast-moving 20th century, she has proved that distance can be a source of royal strength.

So what does the legacy of Elizabeth II, and the way monarchy evolved under her, indicate about the coming reigns of Charles III, William V and, eventually, George VII? If the Elizabethan age is anything to go by (and it is), the monarchy of the future will be smaller, older, cannier, funnier, more reticent and micromanaged, underdressed in private moments and lavish in public ceremonial, more informal but not more intimate. Royalty will appear more middle class, while being nothing of the sort. It will be run on business lines. Under Elizabeth, monarchy has just about broken even, but that has set up expectations of royal solvency; henceforth, it will have to show stakeholders a clear cultural profit.

The problems in Elizabeth's reign have come when modernity has collided with what the Victorian writer Walter Bagehot called the mystery and magic of "the charm of royalty". The family has suffered the sort of problems that afflict most other families: bereavement, failed marriages, younger members behaving badly. Yet whereas the deference of the first half of the century would have ensured such events were treated with decorum and euphemism, the insatiable curiosity of the second half of the 20th century and the start of the 21st meant that those moments have been scrutinised with brutal intensity.

As a consequence, the modern monarchy has become adept at presentational skills and the alchemy of public relations in a way that would have been unthinkable a generation ago. The key strategy (almost a mission statement) is now to enable the monarchy to appear more like the rest of us, while maintaining its mystery. The Duchess of Cambridge is the perfect embodiment of this approach, being university educated, well dressed, decorous, decorative and part of a middle-class family that appears almost quintessentially un-exotic and unthreatening. She has brilliantly absorbed the lessons of Elizabeth II's reign: smile, laugh even, put everyone at ease, say nothing controversial, and wear jeans as easily as a tiara.

There are now enough male royal heirs to last a century, and the future kings will have plenty of time to rehearse. To judge from the longevity of the Windsor bloodline, and based on actuarial calculations, William will be in his sixties before he wears the crown; George is likely to be even older.

When she succeeded her father, the 25-year-old Elizabeth was almost unknown to the British public. Even her nanny, Marion Crawford, who supposedly "told all" in 1950, told very little. Our future monarchs will be exceptionally well known to us by the time they succeed. What they do *before* becoming kings will matter just as much as what they do on the throne.

Older monarchs may have experience and maturity; the disadvantage is that with age come opinions. Queen Elizabeth has resolutely avoided intruding on politics; her son has shown no such self-restraint, insisting, in his own words, that he is "determined not to be confined to cutting ribbons". Perhaps the central question of the monarchy's future is the extent to which the institution can afford to become political. Too outspoken, and it risks fomenting division and controversy; too reticent, and it risks irrelevance.

Ever since the reign of Athelstan, who became the first king of all England in AD925, the British monarchy has survived by giving the impression that it remains a still point in a moving world, a bastion of tradition but adaptable with it. Elizabeth has maintained that illusion. Yet her successors will be required to be moving points in a world that is itself moving at staggering speed, transformed by global influences on British society, economic transition, social and ethnic migrations and radical institutional reform. Our national identity, so static and predictable at the time of Elizabeth's accession, is now in violent flux.

We are long past the time when monarchy could expect to be loved and revered simply for being, for the accident of breeding. It is a cliché to talk of a monarchy "winning" the respect of its people, but Elizabeth's reign has demonstrated just how easily even a popular queen can lose monarchy's popular purchase — and win it again. This is a judgmental, demanding and overachieving age. The next generation of monarchs will have to do something more admirable than the run-of-the-mill royal activity: write something, explore something, prove something or achieve something. Some are born great, some have greatness thrust upon them; the next generation of royals will have to work harder for greatness than any before it.

Queen Elizabeth may come to be seen as the most successful monarch in British history, if success is measured by problems overcome, stability maintained and succession secured. She will leave a monarchy that is still recognisable, but also transformed, and certain to change yet more. Her subtle force of personality has kept the royal ship afloat; for her heirs, royal rule will also be a test of character and resolve.

Perhaps the most important aspect of Elizabeth's legacy will be the ethic of hard work, deep in old age. To live up to this shining example, her heirs will have to work their royal socks off.

▶ **Job done**
Leaving Heathrow after her official opening of Terminal 5 in March 2008

The longest reign

From the unravelling of DNA to a British man winning Wimbledon: in seven decades on the throne the Queen has seen it all

1950s

1953
◆ Street parties are held all over Britain to celebrate the Queen's Coronation, lifting the mood of postwar austerity.
◆ James Watson, Maurice Wilkins, Francis Crick and Rosalind Franklin uncover the structure of DNA.

1954
◆ Rationing is abolished.
◆ Roger Bannister runs the first mile in under four minutes.

1955
◆ Winston Churchill resigns as prime minister.
◆ Ruth Ellis is the last woman to be hanged in Britain.
◆ The Queen opens "The Queen's Building", the former Terminal Two of London Airport, now called Heathrow.

1956
◆ The Clean Air Act begins moves towards a cleaner environment.
◆ The Suez crisis. Anglo-French forces invade Egypt after Egypt's decision to nationalise the Suez Canal Company, but the forces withdraw in the face of international pressure.
◆ Britain's first nuclear power station, Calder Hall, opens in Cumberland.

1957
◆ Anthony Eden resigns as prime minister over Suez.
◆ Britain starts testing its first hydrogen bombs over Christmas Island.
◆ The Queen's Christmas broadcast is televised for the first time.

1958
◆ The Campaign for Nuclear Disarmament (CND) is formed in the wake of widespread fear of nuclear conflict.
◆ First life peerages introduced.
◆ BOAC begins the first transatlantic passenger jet service from London to New York.

1959
◆ The first complete motorway (M1) opens, linking London to Birmingham.
◆ The Mini is launched.

1960s

1960
◆ Britain joins the European Free Trade Association.
◆ Lego arrives in Britain.

1963
◆ The secretary of state for war John Profumo resigns after lying to the House of Commons about his affair with the 19-year-old showgirl Christine Keeler, who was also involved with a Soviet naval attaché.

1964
◆ Britain grants first licences to drill for North Sea oil and gas.
◆ The Rolling Stones and Dusty Springfield appear on the first *Top of the Pops*.

1965
◆ Winston Churchill dies aged 90.
◆ The comprehensive education system is initiated.
◆ The Post Office Tower, now the BT Tower, is opened.
◆ The Queen awards the Beatles MBE medals.

1966
◆ England win the football World Cup.

1967
◆ The Sexual Offences Act is passed, decriminalising homosexuality between men over 21 in England and Wales.

1969
◆ British troops are sent to Northern Ireland after three days of intense violence in Bogside, Londonderry.
◆ The death penalty for murder is abolished in Britain.
◆ Concorde, the world's first supersonic airliner, makes its maiden flight.
◆ Man goes to the Moon. An estimated 530 million people watch Neil Armstrong's giant leap for mankind.

1970s

1970
◆ The Equal Pay Act is introduced prohibiting discrimination between men and women in terms of conditions and pay.
◆ The minimum age for voting is lowered from 21 to 18.

1971
◆ The first British soldier is killed by the IRA.
◆ Decimal currency launches in the UK.

1972
◆ Bloody Sunday. On January 30, British troops open fire on civil rights protesters in Londonderry, Northern Ireland, killing 13 civilians and injuring 17.
◆ Miners' strike and power crisis — state of emergency declared.
◆ The school leaving age is raised to 16.

1973
◆ Britain joins the European Economic Community (EEC).

1974
◆ The government introduces the three-day week to conserve electricity in response to the miners' strike.
◆ The general election ends in a hung parliament with Harold Wilson as prime minister. A second election is held in October and Labour wins with a majority of three.

1975
◆ Britain holds a referendum on its membership of the EEC after renegotiating its terms of entry, and 67 per cent vote in favour of staying in.
◆ Margaret Thatcher becomes leader of the Conservative Party.

1976
◆ The Queen sends her first email.
◆ Concorde completes its first scheduled flight, from Heathrow to Bahrain.

1977
◆ The Queen celebrates her Silver Jubilee by embarking on a three-month tour with the Duke of Edinburgh, visiting 36 counties across Britain and Northern Ireland.

1978
◆ The world's first test-tube baby, Louise Brown, is born.
◆ The prime minister James Callaghan uses the term "winter of discontent" in a speech about widespread public-sector strikes.

1979
◆ Margaret Thatcher becomes Britain's first female prime minister.
◆ The Queen's cousin Earl Mountbatten is killed by an IRA bomb on his boat in Co Sligo, Ireland.

1980s

1980
◆ Britain enters recession. Unemployment rises sharply and reaches two million.

1981
◆ The "Gang of Four" Roy Jenkins, David Owen, Shirley Williams and Bill Rodgers leave Labour to from the new Social Democratic Party (SDP).
◆ Marcus Sarjeant, 19, fires six blanks at the Queen during Trooping the Colour.
◆ Serious rioting in Brixton, south London, follows the arrest of a local black man and sparks violent unrest across England.
◆ The Prince of Wales marries Lady Diana Spencer at St Paul's Cathedral. An estimated 750 million tune in to watch.

1982
◆ Argentina invades and occupies the Falkland Islands, claiming sovereignty over the remote British colony. The bitter conflict lasts ten weeks before Argentina surrenders.
◆ Michael Fagan breaks into Buckingham Palace. He enters the Queen's bedroom and wakes her to ask for some cigarettes. She calmly talks to him before guards arrive.

1983
◆ The IRA bombs the Grand Hotel, Brighton during the Conservative Party conference, killing five. Margaret Thatcher narrowly escapes the blast.
◆ A 12-month miners' strike over pit closures begins.

1985
◆ The British Antarctic Survey discovers the hole in the ozone layer.
◆ Live Aid at Wembley Stadium raises millions for the Ethiopian famine.

1986
◆ Prince Andrew marries Sarah Ferguson at Westminster Abbey; the couple are made the Duke and Duchess of York.
◆ British Gas shares are floated on London stock market at an unexpectedly high premium.

1987
◆ The Great Storm sweeps through southern England.
◆ The *Herald of Free Enterprise* capsizes moments after leaving the Belgian port of Zeebrugge, killing 193 passengers and crew.
◆ An IRA bomb kills 11 during a Remembrance Day ceremony in Enniskillen, Co Fermanagh.
◆ Michael Ryan shoots 31 people, killing 16 including his mother, before committing suicide, in Hungerford, Berkshire.
◆ Fire breaks out at King's Cross Tube station in London, killing 31 people.

1988
◆ A terrorist attack on transatlantic flight Pan Am 103 kills 270 people, 43 of whom are British, when it explodes over the Scottish town of Lockerbie. It begins a 15-year-long battle for justice, with the Libyan leader Colonel Gaddafi eventually claiming responsibility in 2003.
◆ The Liberal Democrats are formed when the SDP merges with the Liberal Party.
◆ An explosion on the Piper Alpha oil platform in the North Sea leaves 167 dead.
◆ Professor Stephen Hawking's *A Brief History of Time* is published.

1990s

1990
◆ A rally over the proposed introduction of the Community Charge — "Poll Tax" — erupts into the worst riots in London for a century.
◆ Margaret Thatcher resigns and is succeeded by John Major.

1991
◆ British forces join in the war to liberate Kuwait from Saddam Hussein's Iraq occupation.

1992
◆ Black Wednesday: the government is forced to withdraw the pound from the ERM, losing £3.14 billion.
◆ Fire spreads from the Queen's private chapel in Windsor Castle throughout much of the building. More than £35 million of repairs are needed.

1993
◆ The Queen starts to pay income tax.
◆ The World Wide Web is launched.
◆ Buckingham Palace opens to the public to raise funds for repairs to Windsor Castle.
◆ Teenager Stephen Lawrence dies after being stabbed in Eltham, southeast London.
◆ The UK Independence Party is established.

1994
◆ The Channel Tunnel opens.
◆ The IRA declares a ceasefire in Northern Ireland.
◆ The National Lottery is launched.
◆ The Church of England ordains its first women priests.

1996
◆ Thomas Hamilton shoots and kills 16 children and one teacher at Dunblane Primary School. New gun laws make private ownership of almost all handguns illegal in Britain.
◆ Dolly the Sheep is born, the first animal to be cloned from an adult cell.

1997
◆ The Queen launches the British Monarchy's official website.
◆ Tony Blair leads Labour in a historic 179-seat majority, signifying the end of Labour's 18 years in opposition.
◆ Britain hands Hong Kong over to China.
◆ Diana, Princess of Wales, dies in a car accident in Paris.
◆ Scotland and Wales vote for devolution.
◆ The Royal Yacht *Britannia* is decommissioned.

1998
◆ The UK and US launch a three-day bombing campaign on Iraqi military targets in response to Saddam Hussein's continued refusal to co-operate with UN weapons inspectors.
◆ The Real IRA sets off a car bomb in Omagh, Northern Ireland, killing 31, the highest death toll from a single incident during the Troubles.
◆ The Good Friday Agreement between Northern Ireland's nationalists and unionists is reached.

1999
◆ The single European currency, the euro, is born.
◆ The UK sees its first total solar eclipse since 1927.
◆ The House of Lords Act ends the centuries-long automatic inclusion of hereditary peers.
◆ The world's population reaches six billion.

2000s

2000
◆ The Freedom of Information Act is passed, giving the public access to information held by public bodies.

2001
◆ Al-Qaeda terrorists bring down the Twin Towers of the World Trade Center in New York.
◆ An outbreak of foot-and-mouth disease causes the worldwide ban on all British exports of livestock, meat and animal products.
◆ Britain joins the US in strikes against the Taliban in Afghanistan in retaliation for the terrorist attacks of 9/11.

2002
◆ Queen Elizabeth the Queen Mother dies at the age of 101. She is given a state funeral during which Westminster Abbey's tenor bell sounds 101 times. The Queen's sister, Princess Margaret, had died less than two months earlier.
◆ The Queen celebrates her Golden Jubilee.

2003
◆ Britain and the US go to war against Saddam Hussein's Iraq.

2004
◆ Kelly Holmes takes gold in the 800m and 1500m at the Athens Olympics.

2010s

2005
◆ The Prince of Wales marries Camilla Parker Bowles in a civil ceremony at the Windsor Guildhall.
◆ YouTube, a video-sharing site, launches. The first video is of the co-founder at the zoo.
◆ July 7 bombings in London.
◆ Civil partnerships are introduced, giving same-sex couples legal recognition of their relationships.

2006
◆ The Queen gives her annual Christmas message live for the first time since 1960. In it she stresses the importance of an inclusive society.

2007
◆ Tony Blair steps down and Gordon Brown succeeds him as prime minister.

2008
◆ The global financial crisis plunges the UK into recession.

2009
◆ Scandal erupts over MPs' expenses claims.

2010
◆ David Cameron becomes PM, leading a Conservative-Liberal Democrat coalition.

2011
◆ The Queen is the first British monarch to visit Ireland since independence.
◆ Thousands riot in cities and towns across England, the violence sparked by a protest over the police shooting of Mark Duggan in Tottenham.

2012
◆ The Queen celebrates her Diamond Jubilee.
◆ London hosts the Olympic Games for the third time.

2013
◆ Lady Thatcher dies aged 87 after a suffering a stroke.
◆ Andy Murray becomes the first Briton to win the Wimbledon men's singles title for 77 years.
◆ Scientists discover the "God particle".

2014
◆ Scotland votes no to independence.
◆ The Queen sends her first tweet from the Science Museum, signing it "Elizabeth R".

2015
◆ The Conservatives win a 12-seat majority despite polling figures predicting a hung parliament.
◆ Elizabeth II becomes the longest-serving monarch in British history.
◆ The House of Commons votes in favour of airstrikes in Syria.

2016
◆ Tim Peake becomes Britain's first European Space Agency astronaut on the International Space Station. After receiving a message of congratulations from the Queen, he replies: "I'm not sure this has ever been said in space before, but I'll be the first: God save the Queen."